Buying and Selling

UNITED STATES COINS

by KEN BRESSETT

An illustrated valuation guide of all regular mint issues from 1792 to date.

Including: historical notes, collector's guide, mintage figures, condition grades, and special sections on commemorative coins, gold, modern proof sets and paper money.

 **Whitman Coin Products**

Copyright © 1982 by

WESTERN PUBLISHING COMPANY, INC.

RACINE, WISCONSIN 53404

9052-13   ISBN: 0-307-90520-9   PRINTED IN U.S.A.

KENNETH E. BRESSETT

Mr. Bressett's numismatic expertise is extensive. For the past twenty years he has served as coordinating editor of R.S. Yeoman's *Guide Book of United States Coins* and the *Handbook of United States Coins* published by Whitman Coin Products, a division of Western Publishing Company, Inc. He has also co-authored several collectors' reference books, among them *Alaska's Coinage Through the Years, Hawaiian Coins, Tokens and Paper Money, Let's Collect Coins, The Fantastic 1804 Dollar,* and *Buying and Selling United States Coins*. In 1962 he authored *The Guide Book of English Coins* which is now in its 9th edition and is used throughout the world. It offers the collector price information, historical data, and mint records of all English coins from 1797 to date.

In addition, Mr. Bressett has written many articles for the coin collecting hobby and served as Managing Editor of the monthly "Whitman Numismatic Journal" from 1964 through 1968. Recognized internationally as one of the leading authorities in the field of numismatics, he has done extensive research on Early American coins.

In 1977 he coordinated the editing and publishing of the American Numismatic Association's Grading Standards book and each year serves as an instructor on the subject at the A.N.A. Summer Seminar.

A popular speaker, Bressett has addressed coin clubs throughout the country for the past thirty years. He is a life member of the American and Canadian Numismatic Associations, as well as a Fellow of the American Numismatic Society and the Royal Numismatic Society of England. In 1966 he was appointed by President Lyndon B. Johnson to serve on the United States Annual Assay Commission.

ARE YOUR COINS GENUINE . . .

Coin authentication and certification service is available for a fee through the American Numismatic Association. Coins must not be submitted without first requesting mailing instructions and a schedule of fees charged for this service. Inquiries about coin authentication should be accompanied by a self-addressed stamped envelope and sent to:

A.N.A. Certification Service
818 N. Cascade
Colorado Springs, Colorado 80903

INTRODUCTION

This book contains all of the essential information needed to collect, buy, and sell United States coins. It is written for the layman who wishes to become a serious collector, as well as for the casual accumulator who wants to know the current value of coins and which of them are worth saving or selling.

A careful reading of the introduction and the historical data will provide all of the basic facts needed to fully understand United States coins and current market values.

The importance of dates, mint marks, and condition cannot be overstated. Information concerning these details should be studied thoroughly. In this book, the term "buying" refers to prices a dealer will pay and the terms "selling" or "retail" to prices dealers charge.

The buying values are an accurate reflection of current prices paid by dealers throughout the country for coins needed for their stock. All prices are averages and are presented only as a matter of information. Actual price quotations may vary from dealer to dealer. The same is true of the selling prices charged by most dealers for their coins. The two sets of prices are shown so that collectors can see which coins are apt to become more valuable as demand and scarcity increase. For a more detailed study of this subject we recommend *A Guide Book of United States Coins* (the Red Book), by R. S. Yeoman, which lists current dealer prices of all United States coins in up to seven grades of condition and the *Handbook of United States Coins* (the Blue Book), also by R. S. Yeoman, which provides similar coverage of prices paid by dealers. Whitman's *Let's Collect Coins,* a companion booklet by Ken Bressett, gives additional information on how to form a collection, the hobby in general, how coins are made, and special terms used by collectors. *Buying and Selling United States Coins* combines the essential parts of these more advanced books and presents the information in easy-to-use form that tells both sides of the coin hobby.

The publisher of this book *does not* buy, sell, or appraise coins. To obtain firm quotations on specific coins, you should consult a dealer engaged in that business. Names of active coin dealers can easily be found in your local telephone directory or in advertisements in periodical coin publications.

IMPORTANT NOTICE

Common date silver coins are valued according to the prevailing price of silver bullion. The values shown for such coins in this edition are based on a spot price of approximately $8.00 per ounce of silver and are shown in italic numbers.

In the event of a change in the price of silver bullion, the approximate value of these coins may be calculated by multiplying the current spot price of silver times the content for each coin as indicated below.

Dealers generally purchase common silver coins at 15-20% below bullion value, and sell them at 15% above bullion value.

The following chart will help to determine the bullion value of common silver coins at various price levels.

Spot Price of Silver Bullion	Dime .07234 oz.	Quarter .18084 oz.	Half Dollar .36169 oz.	Silver Clad Half Dollar .14792 oz.	Dollar .77344 oz.
$ 4.00	$ .29	$ 72	$1.45	$ .59	$ 3.09
4.50	.33	.81	1.63	.67	3.48
5.00	.36	.90	1.81	.74	3.87
5.50	.40	1.00	1.99	.81	4.25
6.00	.44	1.09	2.17	.89	4.64
6.50	.47	1.18	2.35	.96	5.03
7.00	.51	1.27	2.53	1.04	5.42
7.50	.55	1.36	2.72	1.11	5.80
8.00	.58	1.45	2.90	1.19	6.19
8.50	.62	1.54	3.08	1.26	6.58
9.00	.65	1.63	3.26	1.33	6.96
9.50	.69	1.72	3.44	1.42	7.35
10.00	.72	1.81	3.62	1.48	7.73
11.00	.80	1.99	3.98	1.63	8.51
12.00	.87	2.17	4.34	1.78	9.28
13.00	.94	2.35	4.70	1.92	10.05
14.00	1.01	2.53	5.06	2.07	10.83
15.00	1.09	2.71	5.43	2.22	11.60
16.00	1.16	2.89	5.79	2.37	12.38
17.00	1.23	3.07	6.15	2.51	13.15
18.00	1.30	3.26	6.51	2.66	13.92
19.00	1.37	3.44	6.87	2.81	14.70
20.00	1.45	3.62	7.23	2.96	15.47
21.00	1.52	3.80	7.60	3.11	16.24
22.00	1.59	3.98	7.96	3.25	17.02
23.00	1.66	4.16	8.32	3.40	17.79

The value of gold coins listed in this book may be similarly affected by the rise or fall in the price of gold bullion. Values shown for common gold coins are based on a spot price of $375 to $400 per ounce of gold. Nearly all U.S. gold coins have an additional numismatic value beyond their bullion content, and thus are not subject to the minor variations described above for silver coins.

GUIDE TO UNITED STATES COINS

Coins as a Hobby

Coin collecting is perhaps the world's oldest hobby. It has given enjoyment to millions of people who find it relaxing, educational, and profitable. No special talent or knowledge is necessary to collect and enjoy coins, although, as with any endeavor, the more one learns about the subject, the greater are the rewards.

Saving coins can be profitable for the person who knows exactly which coins are valuable and which may become valuable in the future. Early dates are not necessarily the most costly; many modern coins are worth far more than older pieces. Value depends upon the scarcity of the date, where it was minted, and its condition. Collector appeal and factors concerning varieties also have a bearing on price. All of this is explained in detail in this book and should be read with care.

Many coins available in circulation are of value to collectors and dealers. The secret of finding these lies in knowing what to look for. The majority of coins in daily use are silverless "clad" pieces minted since 1965 and cents and nickels minted after 1958. With few exceptions, these are collected only by beginners and will not be purchased by dealers. Coins that have a premium are those not so abundant and pieces in exceptionally nice condition. All silver coins are worth a premium for their bullion value and some have an added collector value. Comparison of the condensed mintage records with buying and selling prices shown for each coin will give a good indication of which dates should be held for immediate or future profit.

Readers will note that some coins with a substantial retail value have little or no wholesale value. Dealers report that they generally have a full supply of these dates and have no need to purchase more. These coins are usually worth holding for future appreciation, when demand exceeds supply. Many times collectors fail to retain such pieces, though they may become more valuable than the scarcer dates that are more often preserved.

In forming a collection of coins you should start by saving one of each date and mint mark. These can be neatly organized in special coin boards or albums available through most book stores, hobby shops, or coin dealers. A few weeks of searching pocket change and other accumulations will provide most of the common dates needed for a good start. Pieces saved should constantly be replaced by better condition specimens when they are available. Rolls of coins obtained at banks or through other sources will often contain many of the scarcer dates. The more coins one inspects the more likely are the chances of finding what is needed. Occasionally a rare or valuable piece will turn up in this manner, but as a rule these are most often found in older household accumulations. Many friends will be found with "hoards" of silver coins taken from recent circulation, and these, too, are a rich source of needed dates.

Books and Periodicals

The key to success is active participation in the hobby and a knowledge of coins. Many museums have extensive collections that may be examined. Most cities have coin clubs that meet monthly and will offer assistance to new collectors. Books and periodicals are available covering in detail every aspect of numismatics. Most of these can be found in public libraries.

The *Guide Book of United States Coins* and the *Handbook of United States Coins,* both by R. S. Yeoman, are revised annually by Western Publishing Company, Inc., Racine, Wisconsin. This company *does not* buy or sell coins; it publishes these books strictly as an impartial report on current premium and retail prices. Similar Whitman books from Western Publishing Company offer complete listings on paper money and foreign coins.

A weekly or monthly publication on coin collecting will expand one's interest in the hobby and provide contacts with other collectors and dealers. The following is a list of the most popular numismatic newspapers and magazines.

COINage Magazine
17337 Ventura Boulevard
Encino, California 91316

Coin World
P.O. Box 150
Sidney, Ohio 45367

Numismatic News
Iola, Wisconsin 54990

Coins Magazine
Iola, Wisconsin 54990

The Numismatist
P.O. Box 2366
Colorado Springs, Col. 80901
(Published monthly by
American Numismatic
 Assn.)

Buying and Selling

Assembling a collection or profiting from the sale of a "lucky find" is part of the enjoyment of saving coins, but each takes time, work, and tenacity. Rarities worth thousands of dollars are not easy to find, but all of the coins priced in this book are available and waiting to be identified in some collection or accumulation. Whether you are buying or selling, the valuation guides shown here will be helpful in determining fair prices. Professional dealers pay for coins according to their needs, and premium values shown are averages of quotations from over sixty leading experts. Average retail prices have been determined by the same method. When purchasing coins for your collection from fellow collectors or friends, a price somewhere between wholesale and retail may be negotiated.

Coins you wish to sell should be examined and appraised by a professional dealer selected from advertisements in local or national publications. Do not send coins to a dealer by mail without first receiving written confirmation of his interest. All packages should be registered or insured and must include name and address of sender, sufficient return postage, and a list of coins submitted.

The condition of a coin has an important relation to its value. An experienced dealer can determine the exact condition of any piece and his opinion will establish the price. He will also determine if coins are counterfeit or have been altered in any way. Coin dealers purchase common silver coins in quantity for their bullion value. The prevailing market for raw silver determines the price, which is much higher than face value. These coins are ultimately melted and sold to industry.

Rolls and complete sets of coins are not necessarily worth more than their total component parts. Many dealers have quantities of common and semi-scarce coins and pay premium prices only for the scarcest dates or "key" coins. Some dealers conduct coin auctions and will sell a customer's coins on a commission basis.

Condition, Preservation, and Cleaning

Coins in top condition are always worth more than inferior or worn specimens. It is therefore important to select the finest possible grade and to provide proper storage to prevent any possible damage from scratching, nicks, or handling. Special coin holders, albums, and envelopes offer suitable protection, provided these are stored in a dry place. Polluted air or a humid atmosphere can cause coins to tarnish, pit, and corrode. Coins taken directly from circulation have been rubbed free of tarnish. Stored for a few months, they turn slightly darker from a light coating of oxidation. Unless this tarnish is excessive, it will do no harm and will, in fact, protect the surface from further change.

Valuable coins should never be cleaned except by an expert. Cleaning seldom improves a coin and usually decreases its value considerably. Dealers will rarely purchase coins that have been cleaned; therefore it is advisable to leave them as they are. Light surface dirt can sometimes be removed by careful washing in soap and water, but rubbing and abrasives will cause damage. Valuable coins should only be held by the edge.

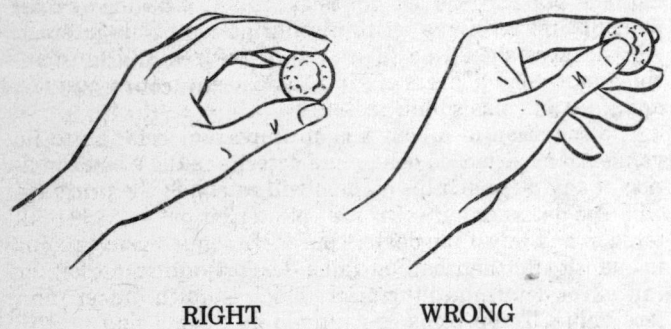

RIGHT   WRONG

The approximate condition of a coin can be determined by referring to the special notations at the beginning of each coin series. For complete details on this subject, the standard reference book is the *American Numismatic Association's Grading Standards for United States Coins*.

Uncirculated coins are those which show absolutely no signs of wear, nicks, scratches, or abrasions. These can be obtained from bank bags, rolls of new coins, directly from the mint in the year of issue, or from old collections. Nearly all uncirculated coins minted prior to 1964 have a value well above prices shown here for circulated specimens. *All* uncirculated coins have a potential premium value and should be saved.

Proof coins are highly polished pieces made especially for collectors, and can be identified by their brilliant mirrorlike finish. They are manufactured by the government on special equipment and sold in sets to the public. A set consists of one coin of each denomination. These coins are sold by the producing mint only during the year of issue and are never released for general circulation at face value. Older sets and individual coins can be purchased only from collectors or dealers.

Mints and Mint Marks

Throughout the years most United States coins have been made at the government mint in Philadelphia. On several occasions branch mints in other cities have assisted in production. Each of the branch mints has been assigned a special mint mark that appears on all of its coinage, but Denver (mint mark D) and San Francisco (mint mark S) are the only branches now in operation. Locations of mint marks are described in this book under each respective coin type. Date listings indicate which mint letter appears on the coins. Normal coins without a mint mark were made at Philadelphia. When evaluating a coin, it is important that the date, mint mark, and condition are correctly identified.

Examples of mint marks—on the reverse of Roosevelt dime prior to 1965, and above date thereafter.

Coins are manufactured on huge machines that impress the design on both sides with a single blow. The special edge reeding used on dimes, quarters, halves and dollars is formed at the same time. Coinage blanks fed into the presses are prepared from alloys or clad composition materials as described under various listings in this book.

Finished coins are distributed to local banks through the Federal Reserve System. All United States coins are legal tender and worth face value, regardless of when they were made. The only exceptions are trade dollars (demonetized in 1887) and gold coins (demonetized in 1933). Gold pieces are not illegal to own. Restrictions on importation, quantity held, and foreign gold coins made after 1933 were removed in 1975.

Weight, edge style, composition, and design of United States coins are established by law. Any deviation is a likely sign of a counterfeit coin. Coinage figures cited here are taken from official government records. All pieces known to exist are included in these listings.

Unusual Coins

Coins illustrated and described in this book cover all regular issues of the United States, all gold coins, and all commemorative pieces made to honor important persons, places, or events. Commemoratives were distributed through banks or special agents and are rarely found in circulation.

All coinage types (major designs) are pictured in exact size. Significant varieties (those with a slight change in design) are listed in each series. Minor varieties are also included when there is a substantial price difference. Overdates, for example, are of added interest because one date has been superimposed upon another. Misstruck coins are not included, as they can only be appraised by a professional.

The 1942 over 1 dime overdate.

Items not found in this catalog fall into three categories: (1) Foreign coins. These usually have the name of the country in the native language, a date, and denomination. The following books will help to identify most of these pieces: *Modern World Coins* (listings from 1850 to 1964) and *Current Coins of the World* (listings from 1964 to date), both by R. S. Yeoman; (2) Tokens issued privately for local use, and (3) Medals made for commemorative or souvenir purposes. Some of these are of value and an experienced collector or dealer can usually help with identification. Information about paper money can be found in Whitman's *A Guide Book of Modern United States Currency* by Neil Shafer.

For a thorough coverage of early Colonial American coins, privately made gold coins of the Gold Rush days, and tokens issued during the Civil War (cent size pieces dated 1861-1864), see Whitman's *Guide Book of United States Coins,* popularly known as the Red Book.

Summary

When using this catalog, keep in mind the importance of correctly identifying the date, mint mark, and condition of each coin. Information and photographs concerning these features are given at the beginning of every coin type listing.

Values shown are averages of prices used by dealers throughout the country and may vary according to dealers' needs. "Buying" values show what a dealer can be expected to pay for wanted coins. "Retail" or "selling" values indicate what he may charge. A dotted line (...) indicates that the coin is worth only face value. Certain very rare pieces have not been evaluated because of infrequent sales. The publisher of this book *does not* buy or sell coins and presents this information only as a report on current market values.

Mintage figures shown are from government records and have been rounded off to the nearest thousand or million as a guide to relative quantities of each issue.

Historical information given tells about composition, edge design, varieties, engravers, weight, and coinage laws. Coins that do not fit these standards may be counterfeit or altered.

It is possible to buy and sell coins directly through dealers who advertise in coin periodicals. Before sending coins to a dealer, always be certain that he has been advised of your intention to do so and that he is willing to accept the coins for appraisal or purchase. Coins should be sent well wrapped by insured or registered mail. Be sure that an itemized invoice of all coins sent is enclosed with the package and that a duplicate is kept for your records. A dealer will generally examine all such shipments and make an offer to purchase them. Coins would be held by him until the offer is accepted or rejected. Return postage and registration fee should always accompany each shipment. When purchasing coins it is proper to write to the dealer describing exactly the type of coin that you wish to buy. If the dealer has offered this coin for sale at a stated price, a check for this amount should be enclosed.

MINTS AND MINT MARKS

Coins struck at Philadelphia prior to 1979 (except 1942 to 1945 five-cent pieces) do not carry a mint mark. The mint mark is now used on all coins except the cents made at Philadelphia. It is a small letter, usually found on the reverse side; the Lincoln cent is an early exception to this. All coins minted after 1967 have the mint mark on the obverse. The letters that signify the various mints are as follows:

    C — Charlotte, North Carolina (gold coins only). 1838-1861.
  CC — Carson City, Nevada. 1870-1893.
    D — Dahlonega, Georgia (gold coins only). 1838-1861.
    D — Denver, Colorado. 1906 to date.
    O — New Orleans, Louisiana. 1838-1909.
    P — Philadelphia, Pennsylvania. 1793 to date.
    S — San Francisco, California. 1854 to date.

All dies for United States coins are made at the Philadelphia Mint. Dies for use at branch mints are hand stamped with the appropriate mint mark before they are shipped from Philadelphia. Because of this hand operation, the exact positioning and size of the mint mark may vary slightly, depending on where and how deeply the punch was impressed. This also accounts for double-punched and superimposed mint marks such as the 1938 D over D, and D over S Buffalo nickels. Polishing of dies may also alter the apparent size of fine details. Occasionally the mint mark is inadvertently left off a die sent to a branch mint, as was the case with some of the 1968 and 1970 proof dimes, and the 1971 proof nickel.

Prior to 1900, punches for mint marks varied greatly in size. This is particularly noticeable in the 1850 to 1880 period in which the letters range from very small to very large. An attempt to standardize sizes started in 1892 with the Barber series, but exceptions are seen in the 1892 O half dollar and 1905 O dime, both of which have normal and "microscopic" mint marks. A more or less standard size small mint mark was used on all minor coins starting in 1909, and on all dimes, quarters and halves after the Barber series was replaced in 1916. Slight variations in mint mark size occur through 1940 with notable differences in 1928, when small and large S mint marks were used.

In recent years a single D or S punch has been used to mark all branch mint dies. The change to the larger D for Denver coins occurred in 1933. Dimes, half dollars and dollars of 1934 exist with either the old, smaller size mint mark or the new, larger size D. All other denominations of 1934 and after are standard. The San Francisco mint mark was changed to its present larger size during 1941 and, with the exception of the half dollar, all 1941 S coins are known with either small or large size mint mark. Halves were not changed until 1942, and the 1942 S pieces exist both ways. The 1945 S dime with "microscopic" S is an unexplained abnormality. New style mint marks were introduced late in 1979.

PROOF COINS

A "proof" is a specimen striking of coinage for presentation, souvenir, exhibition, or numismatic purposes. Pre-1968 proofs were made only at the Philadelphia Mint. Current proofs are made only at San Francisco.

The term "proof" refers to the method of manufacture and not the condition of a coin. Regular production coins in mint state have coruscating frosty luster, soft details, and minor imperfections. Proof coins can usually be distinguished by their sharpness of detail, high wire edge, and extremely brilliant mirrorlike surface. All proofs are originally sold by the mint at a premium.

The Mint's order acceptance for each year's proof coin sets continues until its production limit of these sets has been reached.

All current denominations are included in each proof coin set: a dollar (when minted), half dollar, quarter, dime, nickel and one-cent piece, and these are produced at the San Francisco Assay Office. There is a limit of five sets per order. The price per set is $11.00, including handling and shipment by first class registered mail. Payment, either by check or money order, made payable to the Bureau of the Mint, must accompany each order. Orders for each year's proof coin sets will be filled only during the calendar year. Older sets are not available through the Mint.

All orders for current sets must be mailed to:

>Bureau of the Mint
>55 Mint Street
>San Francisco, California 94175

The above address is now the only address for ordering Mint list medals and special coins, when available.

MODERN PROOF COINS

After a lapse of twenty years, proof coins were struck at the Philadelphia Mint from 1936 to 1942 inclusive. In 1942, when the composition of the five-cent piece was changed, there were two types of this denomination available to collectors. The striking of proof coins was temporarily suspended from 1943 to 1949, and again from 1965 to 1967; during the latter period special mint sets were struck. Proof sets were resumed in 1968. They are delivered from the mint only during the year of issue. Sets from 1936 through 1972 include the cent, nickel, dime, quarter and half; from 1973 through 1981 the dollar was also included.

Figures in parentheses represent the total number of full sets minted.

		Buy	Sell
1936	(3,837)	$4,000	$5,250
1937	(5,542)	2,250	3,000
1938	(8,045)	1,000	1,400
1939	(8,795)	900.00	1,200
1940	(11,246)	800.00	1,000
1941	(15,287)	700.00	900.00
1942 Both nickels	(21,120)	900.00	1,200
1942 One nickel		700.00	900.00

RECENT PROOF SETS

Cent, Nickel, Dime, Quarter, Half
Starting in 1973 sets include the dollar.

	Buy	Sell
1950 .... (51,386)	$400.00	$550.00
1951 .... (57,500)	250.00	350.00
1952 .... (81,980)	135.00	185.00
1953 .... (128,800)	90.00	125.00
1954 .... (233,300)	60.00	85.00
1955 .... (378,200)	50.00	70.00
1956 .... (669,384)	22.00	30.00
1957 .... (1,247,952)	15.00	22.00
1958 .... (875,652)	20.00	30.00
1959 .... (1,149,291)	15.00	22.00
1960 Large date ⎰ (1,691,602)	14.00	20.00
1960 Small date ⎱	25.00	38.00
1961 .... (3,028,244)	9.00	14.00
1962 .... (3,218,019)	9.00	14.00
1963 .... (3,075,645)	9.00	14.00
1964 .... (3,950,762)	9.00	14.00
1968S .... (3,041,506)	3.50	5.50
1969S .... (2,934,631)	3.50	5.50
1970S .... (2,632,810)	8.00	12.00
1971S .... (3,224,138)	3.00	5.00
1972S .... (3,267,667)	3.00	5.00
1973S .... (2,769,624)	7.00	11.00
1974S .... (2,617,350)	6.00	10.00
1975S .... (2,909,369)	11.00	17.00
1976S .... (4,149,730)	5.00	8.00
1976S Three piece set .... (3,295,714)	12.00	19.00
1977S .... (3,251,152)	4.50	7.00
1978S .... (3,127,781)	9.00	14.00
1979S Filled S . ⎰ (3,677,175)	13.00	21.00
1979S Clear S . ⎱	125.00	150.00
1980S .... (3,554,806)	9.00	14.00
1981S .... (4,063,083)	11.00	17.00
1982S	20.00	25.00

SPECIAL MINT SETS

	Buy	Sell
1965 .... (2,360,000)	$3.75	$5.25
1966 .... (2,261,583)	4.00	5.50
1967 .... (1,863,344)	9.00	13.00

TYPICAL GRADING STANDARDS
UNCIRCULATED

Absolutely no trace of wear.

A flawless coin exactly as it was minted, with no trace of wear or injury. Must have full mint luster and brilliance. Any unusual striking or planchet traits must be described.

ABOUT UNCIRCULATED

Small trace of wear visible on highest points.

OBVERSE: Traces of wear show on cheek bone and high points of hair.

REVERSE: Traces of wear show on the beam and triangular roof above pillars.

At least half of the mint luster is still present.

EXTREMELY FINE

Very light wear on only the highest points.

OBVERSE: Hair is lightly worn but well defined and bold. Slight wear shows on cheek bone and bottom of the bust. High points of hair are worn but show all details.

REVERSE: Triangular roof and beam are worn but all details are visible.

VERY FINE

Light to moderate even wear. All major features are sharp.

OBVERSE: Cheek line shows considerable flatness. Over half the hair lines are clear. Parts of the details still show in collar.

REVERSE: Pillars are worn but clearly defined. Triangular roof is partially visible.

FINE

Moderate to heavy even wear. Entire design clear and bold.

OBVERSE: Some details show in hair around face. Cheek line and collar plain but very weak.

REVERSE: Some details visible behind pillars. Triangular roof is very smooth and indistinct.

VERY GOOD

Well worn. Design clear but flat and lacking details.

OBVERSE: Cheek line is visible but parts are worn smooth. Collar is weak but visible. Only a few hair lines show separations.

REVERSE: Slight detail shows throughout building. The arch is worn away. Pillars are weak but visible.

GOOD

Heavily worn. Design and legend visible but faint in spots.

OBVERSE: Entire design well worn with very little detail remaining. Motto is weak and merged with rim.

REVERSE: Building is nearly flat but is well outlined. Pillars are worn flat. Rim worn to tops of letters.

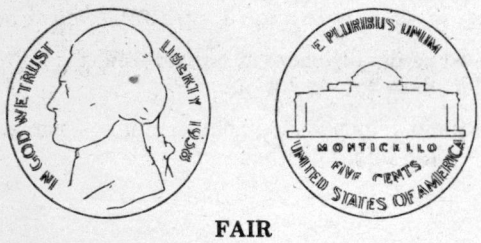

FAIR

Outlined design. Parts of date and legend worn smooth.

OBVERSE: Design is outlined with nearly all details worn away. Date and legend readable but very weak and merging into rim.

REVERSE: Entire design partially worn away. Rim is merged with the letters.

COLONIAL COINAGE

The Articles of Confederation, adopted July 9, 1778, provided that Congress should have the sole right to regulate the alloy and value of coin struck by its own authority or by that of the respective states.

Each state, therefore, had the right to coin money, but Congress served as a regulating authority. New Hampshire was the first state to consider coinage, but few if any coins were placed in circulation.

Vermont, Connecticut, and New Jersey granted coining privileges to companies or individuals. Massachusetts erected its own mint in which copper coins were produced. A number of interesting varieties of these state issues, most of which were struck in fairly large quantities, can still be easily acquired, and form the basis for many present day collections of early American coins.

The first Colonial coins struck in this country were the crude "NE Shillings" by the colony of Massachusetts. These pieces were followed by the famous Massachusetts "Pine Tree Shillings" which are dated 1652; this series also included sixpence and threepence pieces of 1652. Dealers buy the more popular Colonial coins at approximately the following prices.

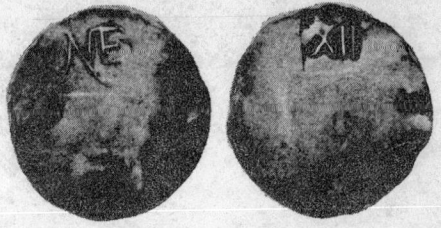

NE Shilling.. $3,500

Massachusetts Pine Tree and Oak Tree Shillings .. $150.00
Pine Tree Sixpence............................... $110.00
Pine Tree Threepence $100.00

1722-1723 Rosa Americana Coppers....... $15.00 to $30.00

1722-1724 Wood's Hibernia Coppers .... $5.00 to $15.00

1773 Virginia Halfpenny .... $4.50 to $15.00

1783-1785 Nova Constellatio Coppers ..... $15.00 to $30.00

THE CONTINENTAL DOLLAR

The Continental Dollar was probably a pattern issue only and never reached general circulation. It was the first silver dollar size coin ever proposed for the United States. The dies were engraved by someone whose initials were E. G. (possibly Elisha Gallaudet). Some of them have his signature "EG FECIT" on the obverse. The coins were probably struck in Philadelphia.

Varieties result from differences in the spelling of the word CURRENCY and the addition of EG FECIT. These coins were struck in silver, pewter and brass, those in silver probably having done service as a dollar.

1776 Continental Dollar $800.00

1785-1788 Connecticut Coppers .... $4.00 to $25.00

1787 New York Coppers .... $15.00 to $150.00

1787-1788 Massachusetts Cent and
Half Cent .... $8.00 to $20.00

1786 to 1788 New Jersey Coppers .... $5.00 to $25.00

 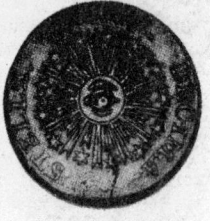

1785 to 1788 Vermont Coppers .... $15.00 to $115.00

1787 Fugio Cent .... $10.00 to $25.00

1783-1795 Washington Head Coppers ..... $12.00 to $50.00

1794-1795 Talbot, Allum and Lee Cent.... $10.00 to $20.00

HALF CENTS 1793-1857

The United States half cent was authorized April 2, 1792, but was not issued until the following year. The denomination was continued until 1857, when both large cents and half cents were replaced by the small size cent. Early pieces weigh 104 grains and have a lettered edge. This was changed to 84 grains after 1795 and the edge lettering discontinued.

This denomination was not minted every year and was issued in limited quantities at the Philadelphia Mint only. All of them are scarce and worth a premium today, even in worn condition. Several minor varieties exist that are of interest to specialists in the series. Pieces dated 1831, 1836, 1840 through 1848, and 1852 were made for collecting purposes only and are very rare.

Liberty Cap Type 1793-1797

Head Left 1793

FAIR—*Clear enough to identify.*
GOOD—*Outline of bust clear, no details. Date readable. Reverse lettering incomplete.*
VERY GOOD—*Some hair details. Reverse lettering complete.*

Date	Thousands Minted	Avg. Dealers Pay Fair	Good	Average Retail Prices Fair	Good	V. Good
1793	35	$300.00	$750.00	$500.00	$1,000	$1,500

Head Right 1794-1797

1794	81	60.00	100.00	90.00	200.00	250.00
1795	134	50.00	90.00	80.00	140.00	225.00
1796	6	625.00	1,200	1,800	3,500	6,000
1797	119	40.00	80.00	60.00	150.00	225.00

HALF CENTS
Draped Bust Type 1800-1808

FAIR—*Clear enough to identify.*
GOOD—*Bust outline clear, no details, date readable. Reverse lettering worn and incomplete.*
VERY GOOD—*Some drapery shows. Date and legend complete.*

Date	Thousands Minted	Avg. Dealers Pay Fair	Good	Average Retail Prices Fair	Good	V. Good
1800	211	$7.00	$15.00	$18.00	$25.00	$35.00
1802	14	50.00	95.00	80.00	175.00	325.00
1803	98	7.00	15.00	20.00	25.00	35.00
1804	1,055	7.00	15.00	16.00	23.00	32.00
1805	814	7.00	15.00	16.00	23.00	32.00
1806	356	7.00	15.00	16.00	23.00	32.00
1807	476	7.00	15.00	16.00	23.00	32.00
1808	400	7.00	15.00	17.00	24.00	35.00

Classic Head Type 1809-1836

GOOD—*LIBERTY only partly visible on hair band. Lettering, date, stars, worn but visible.*
VERY GOOD—*LIBERTY entirely visible on hair band. Lower curls worn.*
FINE—*Only part wear on LIBERTY and hair at top worn in spots.*

Date	Thousands Minted	Avg. Dealers Pay Good	V. Good	Average Retail Prices Good	V. Good	Fine
1809	1,154	14.00	16.00	20.00	25.00	35.00
1810	215	15.00	20.00	25.00	35.00	50.00

HALF CENTS
Classic Head Type 1809-1836

Date	Thousands Minted	Avg. Dealers Pay Good	V. Good	Average Retail Prices Good	V. Good	Fine
1811	63	$30.00	$45.00	$70.00	$95.00	$175.00
1825	63	14.00	17.00	23.00	30.00	40.00
1826	234	14.00	16.00	19.00	23.00	33.00
1828	606	14.00	16.00	19.00	23.00	33.00
1829	487	14.00	16.00	19.00	23.00	33.00
1831	2	Rare				
1832	154	12.00	15.00	19.00	23.00	30.00
1833	120	12.00	15.00	19.00	23.00	30.00
1834	141	12.00	15.00	19.00	23.00	30.00
1835	398	12.00	15.00	19.00	23.00	30.00
1836		Rare				

Braided Hair Type 1840-1857

VERY GOOD—*Beads uniformly distinct. Hairlines show in spots.*
FINE—*Hairlines above ear worn. Beads sharp.*
VERY FINE—*Curls on lower part of neck distinct.*

Date	Thousands Minted	Avg. Dealers Pay V. Good	Fine	Average Retail Prices V. Good	Fine	V. Fine
1840 thru 1848		Rare				
1849	40	16.00	22.00	32.00	37.50	60.00
1850	40	16.00	22.00	32.00	37.50	60.00
1851	148	15.00	20.00	27.50	32.00	55.00
1852		Rare				
1853	129	15.00	20.00	27.50	32.00	55.00
1854	55	15.00	20.00	27.50	32.00	55.00
1855	56	15.00	20.00	27.50	32.00	55.00
1856	40	17.00	22.00	32.00	37.50	60.00
1857	35	18.00	25.00	35.00	40.00	65.00

LARGE CENTS 1793-1857

The United States large cent was authorized in 1792 by the same act that authorized the half cent. Coinage was discontinued in 1857, when the small cent was introduced. All large cents were struck at the Philadelphia Mint and therefore do not have a mint mark. They were coined every year except 1815. Numerous minor varieties exist for every date and some of these are worth an additional premium. Both half cents and large cents were made of nearly pure copper, which wore very rapidly. Early dates in high grade condition are very scarce. 1793-1795 with edge inscription. Plain edge thereafter.

Flowing Hair Type 1793-1796

FAIR—Date and devices clear enough to identify.
GOOD—Lettering worn but readable. Bust has no detail.
VERY GOOD—Date and lettering distinct, some details of head visible.

Date	Thousands Minted	Avg. Dealers Pay Fair	Good	Average Retail Prices Fair	Good	V. Good
1793 Chain	35	$300.00	$900.00	$500.00	$1,500	$2,250

| 1793 Wreath | 63 | 200.00 | 450.00 | 400.00 | 1,000 | 2,000 |

LARGE CENTS

Date	Thousands Minted	Avg. Dealers Pay		Average Retail Prices		
		Fair	Good	Fair	Good	V. Good
1793 Cap	11	$275.00	$475.00	$400.00	$900.00	$1,400
1794	918	25.00	50.00	40.00	75.00	125.00
1795	538	20.00	40.00	30.00	60.00	110.00
1796	110	30.00	50.00	40.00	80.00	150.00

Draped Bust Type 1796-1807

FAIR—*Clear enough to identify.*
GOOD—*Lettering worn, but clear; date clear. Bust lacks details.*
VERY GOOD—*Drapery partly visible. Less wear in date and lettering.*

1796	363	20.00	40.00	35.00	70.00	115.00
1797	897	12.00	18.00	17.00	30.00	45.00
1798	980	9.00	15.00	12.50	22.50	40.00
1799	904	150.00	375.00	250.00	475.00	900.00
1800	2,822	5.00	12.00	7.00	17.00	30.00
1801	1,363	5.00	12.00	7.00	17.00	30.00
1802	3,435	5.00	11.00	7.00	15.00	25.00
1803	2,471	5.00	11.00	7.00	14.00	30.00
1804	757	100.00	200.00	175.00	275.00	525.00
1805	941	5.00	11.00	7.00	14.00	30.00
1806	348	7.00	18.00	10.00	25.00	55.00
1807	727	5.00	11.00	7.00	14.00	30.00

LARGE CENTS
Classic Head Type 1808-1814

FAIR*—Details clear enough to identify.*
GOOD*—Legends, stars, date worn, but plain.*
VERY GOOD*—LIBERTY all readable. Ear shows. Details worn but plain.*

Date	Thousands Minted	Avg. Dealers Pay		Average Retail Prices		
		Fair	Good	Fair	Good	V. Good
1808	1,109	$8.00	$17.00	$12.00	$24.00	$50.00
1809	223	22.00	45.00	35.00	70.00	125.00
1810	1,458	7.00	16.00	11.00	22.50	45.00
1811	218	15.00	32.00	25.00	42.50	80.00
1812	1,075	7.00	16.00	11.00	22.50	45.00
1813	418	10.00	20.00	15.00	35.00	65.00
1814	358	7.00	16.00	11.00	22.50	45.00

GOOD*—Head details partly visible. Even wear in date and legends.*
V. GOOD*—LIBERTY, date, stars, legends clear. Part of hair cord visible.*
FINE*—All hairlines show. Hair cords show uniformly.*

Date	Millions Minted	Avg. Dealers Pay		Average Retail Prices		
		Good	V. Good	Good	V. Good	Fine
1816	2.8	4.50	6.00	7.00	9.00	15.00

LARGE CENTS

Date	Millions Minted	Avg. Dealers Pay Good	V. Good	Average Retail Prices Good	V. Good	Fine
1817	3.9	$4.00	$5.00	$7.00	$9.00	$14.00
1818	3.2	4.00	5.00	7.00	8.00	13.00
1819	2.7	4.00	5.00	7.00	8.00	13.00
1820	4.4	4.00	5.00	7.00	8.00	12.00
1821	0.4	8.00	14.00	15.00	25.00	40.00
1822	2.1	4.50	6.00	7.00	8.00	12.00
1823	0.8	15.00	25.00	25.00	35.00	65.00
1824	1.3	4.50	6.00	8.00	12.00	18.00
1825	1.5	4.00	5.50	7.00	10.00	15.00
1826	1.5	4.00	5.50	7.00	8.00	12.00
1827	2.4	4.00	5.50	7.00	8.00	12.00
1828	2.3	4.00	5.00	7.00	8.00	12.00
1829	1.4	4.00	5.00	7.00	8.00	12.00
1830	1.7	4.00	5.00	7.00	8.00	12.00
1831	3.4	3.75	4.50	6.00	7.50	10.00
1832	2.4	3.75	4.50	6.00	7.50	10.00
1833	2.7	3.75	4.50	6.00	7.50	10.00
1834	1.8	4.00	5.25	7.00	8.00	11.00
1835	3.9	3.75	4.50	6.00	7.50	10.00
1836	2.1	3.75	4.50	6.00	7.50	10.00
1837	5.6	3.75	4.50	6.00	7.50	10.00
1838	6.4	3.75	4.50	6.00	7.50	10.00

Braided Hair Type 1839-1857

Date	Millions Minted	Good	V. Good	Good	V. Good	Fine
1839	3.1	4.00	5.25	7.00	10.00	16.00
1840	2.5	3.75	4.50	6.00	7.50	10.00
1841	1.6	3.75	4.50	6.00	8.00	10.00
1842	2.4	3.75	4.50	6.00	8.00	10.00
1843	2.4	3.75	4.50	6.00	8.00	12.00
1844	2.4	3.75	4.50	6.00	8.00	10.00
1845	3.9	3.50	4.25	6.00	7.00	9.00
1846	4.1	3.50	4.25	7.00	8.00	10.00
1847	6.2	3.50	4.25	6.00	7.00	9.00
1848	6.4	3.50	4.25	6.00	7.00	9.00
1849	4.2	3.50	4.25	6.00	7.00	9.00

LARGE CENTS

Date	Millions Minted	Avg. Dealers Pay Good	V. Good	Average Retail Prices Good	V. Good	Fine
1850	4.4	$3.50	$4.25	$6.00	$7.00	$9.00
1851	9.9	3.50	4.00	6.00	7.00	9.00
1852	5.1	3.50	4.00	6.00	7.00	9.00
1853	6.6	3.50	4.00	6.00	7.00	9.00
1854	4.2	3.50	4.00	6.00	7.00	9.00
1855	1.6	3.75	4.50	6.00	7.00	9.00
1856	2.7	3.75	4.50	6.00	7.00	9.00
1857	0.3	12.00	16.00	22.50	30.00	40.00

FLYING EAGLE CENTS 1856-1858

The small size cents of this period are composed of 88% copper and 12% nickel, and weigh 72 grains. They were authorized by the Act of February 21, 1857. Those dated 1856 were experimental pieces not authorized for general circulation, although they are occasionally found in worn condition. Varieties of the 1858 cent occur with either large or small letters in the legend. All were struck at the Philadelphia Mint.

GOOD—All details worn, but readable.
V. GOOD—Feather details and eye of eagle are evident, but worn.
FINE—Eagle head details and feather tips sharp.

1856		575.00	700.00	825.00	950.00	1,300
1857	17	5.00	6.00	9.00	11.00	15.00
1858	25	5.00	6.00	9.00	11.00	15.00

INDIAN HEAD CENTS

Copper-nickel 1859-1864

Small cents dated 1859 through 1864 were made of the same composition and weight as the Flying Eagle cents. The design was engraved by J. B. Longacre. After 1859 a shield was added to the reverse. All were coined at the Philadelphia Mint.

INDIAN HEAD CENTS

GOOD—*No LIBERTY visible.*
V. GOOD—*At least three letters of LIBERTY readable.*
FINE—*LIBERTY completely visible on headband.*

Date	Millions Minted	Avg. Dealers Pay		Average Retail Prices		
		Good	V. Good	Good	V. Good	Fine
1859	36	$2.25	$2.75	$4.50	$5.75	$11.00

    With shield on reverse

1860	20	2.00	2.70	3.75	5.00	8.75
1861	10	4.00	6.00	8.50	11.50	17.50
1862	28	1.75	2.00	3.25	4.25	6.50
1863	50	1.75	2.00	3.25	4.25	6.50
1864	14	3.00	4.00	6.00	8.25	14.00

Bronze Cents 1864-1909

The size and composition of the small cent was changed in 1864 to an alloy of 95% copper and 5% tin and zinc, with a weight of 48 grains. Longacre's design of the Indian Head was continued until 1909. All pieces were struck at Philadelphia without mint mark until 1908. In that year and in 1909 some pieces were coined at San Francisco and bear a small letter "S" on the reverse to indicate that mint.

1864	39	1.75	2.75	3.00	5.50	8.50
1865	35	1.50	2.25	2.75	4.00	7.50
1866	10	12.00	15.00	17.00	22.00	30.00
1867	10	12.00	15.00	17.00	22.00	30.00
1868	10	12.00	15.00	17.00	22.00	30.00

INDIAN HEAD CENTS

Date	Millions Minted	Avg. Dealers Pay		Average Retail Prices		
		Good	V. Good	Good	V. Good	Fine
1869	6	$18.00	$25.00	$25.00	$35.00	$60.00
1870	5	15.00	20.00	20.00	27.50	50.00
1871	4	18.00	25.00	25.00	35.00	60.00
1872	4	25.00	30.00	35.00	45.00	75.00
1873	12	4.50	6.00	7.00	9.00	16.50
1874	14	4.50	6.00	7.00	9.00	16.50
1875	13	4.50	6.00	7.00	9.00	16.50
1876	8	7.00	9.00	11.00	14.00	25.00
1877	0.9	200.00	225.00	300.00	350.00	450.00
1878	6	7.00	9.00	11.00	14.00	30.00
1879	16	1.15	1.75	2.50	3.50	7.00
1880	39	.70	.90	1.20	1.70	3.60
1881	39	.70	.90	1.20	1.70	3.60
1882	39	.70	.90	1.20	1.70	3.60
1883	46	.70	.90	1.20	1.70	3.60
1884	23	.85	1.40	1.75	3.25	6.00
1885	12	1.75	3.00	3.75	6.50	10.00
1886	17	.85	1.50	2.10	3.25	6.00
1887	45	.50	.60	1.00	1.50	2.25
1888	37	.50	.60	1.00	1.50	2.25
1889	49	.50	.60	1.00	1.50	2.25
1890	57	.50	.60	1.00	1.50	2.25
1891	47	.50	.60	1.00	1.50	2.25
1892	38	.50	.60	1.00	1.50	2.25
1893	47	.50	.60	1.00	1.50	2.25
1894	17	.75	1.35	1.75	3.75	6.75
1895	38	.40	.50	.75	1.00	1.60
1896	39	.40	.50	.75	1.00	1.60
1897	50	.40	.50	.75	1.00	1.60
1898	50	.40	.50	.75	1.00	1.60
1899	54	.40	.50	.75	1.00	1.60
1900	67	.40	.45	.75	.90	1.30
1901	80	.40	.45	.75	.90	1.30
1902	87	.40	.45	.75	.90	1.30
1903	85	.40	.45	.75	.90	1.30
1904	61	.40	.45	.75	.90	1.30
1905	81	.40	.45	.75	.90	1.30
1906	96	.40	.45	.75	.90	1.30
1907	108	.40	.45	.75	.90	1.30
1908	32	.40	.45	.75	.90	1.30
1908S	1	15.00	16.00	20.00	22.00	27.50
1909	14	.50	.65	1.10	1.75	2.40
1909S	0.3	65.00	80.00	100.00	125.00	150.00

Location of mint mark S on reverse of Indian cent (1908 and 1909 only).

LINCOLN CENTS
Wheat Ears Reverse 1909-1958

Cents of this type were coined at the Philadelphia, Denver, and San Francisco Mints. The mint mark is always located beneath the date. The composition is the same as the previous type, with the exception of those made during the war years 1943 through 1945.

In 1909 the designer's initials, VDB (for Victor D. Brenner), were placed on the reverse of some of the coins. Later in the year they were removed from the dies but restored in 1918 as very small incuse letters beneath the shoulder.

Interesting varieties dated 1955, 1969S and 1972 have double lettering and date on the obverse due to faulty preparation of the die. Coins with this feature are very scarce.

Location of mint mark S or D on obverse of Lincoln cent.

Location of designer's initials V.D.B. on 1909 only.

GOOD—Date worn but apparent. Lines in wheat ears missing. Full rims.
VERY GOOD—Half of lines show in upper wheat ears.
FINE—Wheat lines worn but visible.
VERY FINE—Cheek and jaw bones worn but separated. No worn spots on wheat ears.
EXTRA FINE—Slight wear. All details sharp.

Date	Millions Minted	Avg. Dealers Pay Good	V. Good	Average Retail Prices Good	V. Good	Fine
1909 VDB	28	$ .90	$1.10	$1.75	$2.00	$2.50
1909S, VDB	0.5	200.00	225.00	300.00	350.00	400.00

LINCOLN CENTS

Date	Millions Minted	Avg. Dealers Pay Good	V. Good	Average Retail Prices Good	V. Good	Fine
1909	73	$ .12	$ .15	$ .40	$ .45	$ .60
1909S	1.8	25.00	30.00	40.00	45.00	50.00
1910	146	.06	.08	.20	.30	.45
1910S	6	5.00	5.75	6.50	7.50	8.50
1911	101	.06	.10	.20	.30	.60
1911D	12	2.75	3.00	3.00	4.00	5.50
1911S	4	7.25	8.00	10.00	11.00	12.00
1912	68	.06	.14	.25	.40	1.25
1912D	10	3.00	3.25	3.00	4.00	5.75
1912S	4	6.50	7.00	9.00	10.00	12.00
1913	76	.05	.11	.20	.35	1.25
1913D	16	1.00	1.25	1.50	2.00	3.25
1913S	6	4.50	5.50	6.00	7.00	8.00
1914	75	.07	.13	.25	.40	1.70
1914D	1.2	65.00	70.00	85.00	100.00	125.00
1914S	4	5.00	6.00	7.00	9.00	11.00
1915	29	.30	.50	.60	1.00	3.50
1915D	22	.30	.45	.60	1.00	1.50
1915S	5	4.00	4.50	5.00	6.00	7.50
1916	132	.03	.06	.20	.30	.40
1916D	36	.10	.14	.25	.40	.90
1916S	22	.30	.40	.55	1.00	1.50
1917	196	.03	.05	.15	.20	.35
1917D	55	.08	.12	.25	.35	.75
1917S	33	.10	.15	.25	.35	.75
1918	288	.04	.08	.20	.25	.40
1918D	48	.12	.17	.25	.35	.70
1918S	35	.12	.17	.25	.35	.70
1919	392	.03	.06	.20	.25	.40
1919D	57	.10	.15	.25	.35	.70
1919S	140	.07	.13	.25	.35	.50
1920	310	.03	.06	.20	.25	.35
1920D	49	.10	.15	.25	.35	.60
1920S	46	.10	.15	.25	.35	.60
1921	39	.10	.15	.25	.35	.60
1921S	15	.35	.45	.60	.85	1.25
1922D	7	2.60	3.25	4.75	5.75	6.75
1922 no D		140.00	170.00	180.00	235.00	315.00
1923	75	.04	.05	.15	.20	.35
1923S	9	.75	.85	1.40	1.75	2.50
1924	75	.04	.05	.15	.20	.35
1924D	2	6.00	7.50	8.00	10.00	13.00
1924S	12	.25	.40	.60	.80	1.40
1925	140	.04	.05	.15	.25	.35
1925D	22	.10	.15	.30	.40	.60
1925S	26	.08	.12	.25	.35	.55
1926	157	.04	.05	.15	.25	.35

LINCOLN CENTS

Date	Millions Minted	Avg. Dealers Pay Good	V. Good	Average Retail Prices Good	V. Good	Fine
1926D	28	$ .08	$ .12	$ .25	$ .35	$ .60
1926S	4	1.50	1.75	3.00	3.60	5.00
1927	144	.03	.04	.15	.20	.30
1927D	27	.06	.10	.25	.35	.50
1927S	14	.25	.30	.40	.55	.90
1928	134	.03	.04	.15	.20	.30
1928D	31	.05	.07	.20	.30	.40
1928S	17	.12	.17	.25	.35	.60
1929	185	.03	.04	.15	.20	.30
1929D	42	.03	.04	.15	.25	.35
1929S	50	.03	.04	.15	.25	.35
1930	157	.03	.04	.10	.15	.25
1930D	40	.05	.08	.15	.20	.30
1930S	24	.05	.08	.15	.20	.30
1931	19	.15	.20	.25	.35	.45
1931D	4	1.65	1.90	3.00	3.25	4.00
1931S	0.9	20.00	24.00	30.00	33.00	36.00
1932	9	.70	.80	.90	1.25	1.50
1932D	10	.30	.35	.60	.80	1.20
1933	14	.20	.30	.50	.60	.70
1933D	6	1.00	1.15	1.60	1.90	2.25
1934	219	.02	.02	.05	.10	.15
1934D	28	.08	.09	.15	.25	.30
1935	245	.02	.02	.05	.10	.15
1935D	47	.02	.02	.05	.10	.15
1935S	39	.02	.02	.05	.10	.20
1936	310	.02	.02	.95	.10	.15
1936D	41	.02	.02	.05	.10	.20
1936S	29	.02	.03	.05	.10	.25
1937	309	.02	.02	.05	.07	.10
1937D	50	.02	.02	.05	.10	.15
1937S	34	.02	.03	.05	.10	.20
1938	157	.02	.02	.05	.10	.15
1938D	20	.02	.03	.15	.20	.30
1938S	15	.10	.12	.25	.35	.45
1939	316	.02	.02	.05	.07	.10
1939D	15	.05	.10	.35	.45	.55
1939S	52	.02	.02	.10	.15	.20
1940	587	.02	.02	.05	.07	.10
1940D	81	.02	.02	.05	.07	.10
1940S	113	.02	.02	.05	.07	.10
1941	887	.02	.02	.05	.07	.10
1941D	129	.02	.02	.05	.07	.10
1941S	92	.02	.02	.05	.07	.10
1942	658	.02	.02	.05	.07	.10
1942D	207	.02	.02	.05	.07	.10
1942S	86	.02	.02	.07	.10	.15

LINCOLN CENTS
Wartime Steel Cents 1943

During the critical war year of 1943, the Treasury Department resorted to the use of zinc-coated steel for making Lincoln cents. No bronze cents were officially issued in 1943; a few specimens, however, probably struck on bronze planchets, are known to exist. Cents dated 1944 and 1945 were made from salvaged shell cases and are a little lighter in color than those of other dates.

Date	Millions Minted	Avg. Dealers Pay V. Fine	Ex. Fine	Average Retail Prices V. Fine	Ex. Fine	Unc.
1943	685	$ .05	$ .10	$ .25	$ .30	$1.10
1943D	218	.12	.15	.25	.30	2.00
1943S	192	.12	.15	.45	.55	3.50

Bronze Composition Resumed

Date	Millions Minted	V. Fine	Ex. Fine	V. Fine	Ex. Fine	Unc.
1944	1,435	.02	.02	.10	.20	.30
1944D	431	.02	.02	.10	.15	.30
1944S	283	.02	.02	.10	.20	.50
1945	1,040	.02	.02	.10	.15	.35
1945D	226	.02	.02	.10	.20	.70
1945S	182	.02	.02	.10	.20	.50
1946	992	.02	.02	.10	.15	.25
1946D	316	.02	.02	.10	.20	.30
1946S	198	.02	.02	.10	.20	.70
1947	190	.02	.02	.10	.20	.30
1947D	195	.02	.02	.10	.20	.30
1947S	99	.02	.04	.15	.25	.80
1948	317	.02	.02	.10	.20	.60
1948D	173	.02	.02	.10	.20	.30
1948S	82	.02	.04	.15	.30	.90
1949	218	.02	.02	.10	.20	.85
1949D	153	.02	.02	.10	.20	.70
1949S	64	.02	.05	.20	.30	2.00
1950	273	.02	.02	.10	.20	.50
1950D	335	.02	.02	.10	.20	.30
1950S	118	.02	.03	.10	.25	.55
1951	285	.02	.02	.10	.25	1.00
1951D	625	.02	.02	.10	.15	.25
1951S	136	.02	.03	.15	.25	1.25
1952	187	.02	.02	.05	.15	.60
1952D	746	.02	.02	.05	.15	.25
1952S	138	.02	.03	.05	.20	.65
1953	257	.02	.02	.05	.10	.25
1953D	700	.02	.02	.05	.10	.25
1953S	182	.02	.03	.05	.15	.45
1954	72	.02	.05	.25	.35	.50
1954D	251	.02	.02	.05	.10	.25
1954S	96	.02	.04	.05	.20	.35

LINCOLN CENTS

Date	Millions Minted	Avg. Dealers Pay V. Fine	Avg. Dealers Pay Ex. Fine	Average Retail Prices V. Fine	Average Retail Prices Ex. Fine	Average Retail Prices Unc.
1955 Doubled die obverse....		$225.00	$300.00	$350.00	$400.00	$600.00
1955	331	...	.02	...	.10	.20
1955D	563	...	.02	...	.10	.25
1955S	45	.12	.17	.30	.40	.60
1956	421	...	.02	...	.05	.25
1956D	1,098	...	.02	...	.05	.20
1957	284	...	.02	...	.05	.20
1957D	1,051	...	.02	...	.05	.20
1958	253	...	.02	...	.05	.25
1958D	801	...	.02	...	.05	.25

Lincoln Memorial Type 1959 to Date

The reverse of the Lincoln cent was changed in 1959 to commemorate the 150th anniversary of Lincoln's birth. The new design was the work of Frank Gasparro, whose initials FG appear to the right of the monument.

Composition of the cent was changed slightly in 1962 to an alloy of 95% copper and 5% zinc.

Varieties of the 1960 cent from both mints occur with either large or small date.

EXTRA FINE—Lines of ear raised and sharp. Cheek and jaw bones clearly defined although worn.

LINCOLN CENTS

Memorial Reverse 1959 to Date

Date	Millions Minted	Avg. Dealers Pay V. Fine	Ex. Fine	Average Retail Prices V. Fine	Ex. Fine	Unc.
1959	611	...	...	...	...	$ .10
1959D	1,280	...	...	...	...	.10

Small Date | Large Date

1960	588	...	...	...	...	.10
1960 Small date		1.00	1.25	...	...	4.00
1960D	1,580	...	...	...	...	.10
1960D Small date		...	.02	...	...	.30
1961	756	...	...	...	...	.10
1961D	1,753	...	...	...	...	.10
1962	609	...	...	...	...	.10
1962D	1,793	...	...	...	...	.10
1963	757	...	...	...	...	.10
1963D	1,774	...	...	...	...	.10
1964	2,652	...	...	...	...	.10
1964D	3,799	...	...	...	...	.10
1965	1,497	...	...	...	...	.10
1966	2,188	...	...	...	...	.10
1967	3,048	...	...	...	...	.10
1968	1,708	...	...	...	...	.10
1968D	2,886	...	...	...	...	.10
1968S	261	...	...	...	...	.10
1969	1,137	...	...	...	...	.60
1969D	4,003	...	...	...	...	.10
1969S	547	...	...	...	...	.10
1969S Doubled die obverse		...	...	...	...	...
1970	1,898	...	...	...	...	.10
1970D	2,891	...	...	...	...	.10
1970S sm	693	...	...	...	...	10.00
1970S lg		...	...	...	...	.50
1971	1,919	...	...	...	...	.30
1971D	2,911	...	...	...	...	.10
1971S	528	...	...	...	...	.35
1972	2,933	...	...	...	...	.10

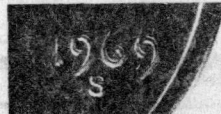

1969S Doubled die obverse | Small Date Numbers aligned at top | Large Date Low 7 in date

LINCOLN CENTS

1972 Doubled die obverse....	...	$110.00	...	325.00
1972D..... 2,665	...	...	...	.10
1972S....... 380	...	...	...	.10
1973...... 3,728	...	...	...	.10
1973D..... 3,550	...	...	...	.10
1973S....... 320	...	...	...	.10
1974...... 4,232	...	...	...	.10
1974D..... 4,235	...	...	...	.10
1974S....... 412	...	...	...	.10
1975...... 5,451	...	...	...	.10
1975D..... 4,505	...	...	...	.10
1975S Proof ... 3		5.00		12.00
1976...... 4,674	...	...	...	.10
1976D..... 4,221	...	...	...	.10
1976S Proof ... 4		2.00		3.75
1977...... 4,470	...	...	...	.10
1977D..... 4,194	...	...	...	.10
1977S Proof ... 3		2.50		3.75
1978...... 5,559	...	...	...	.10
1978D..... 4,280	...	...	...	.10
1978S Proof ... 3		2.50		4.00
1979...... 6,019	...	...	...	.10
1979D..... 4,139	...	...	...	.10
1979S Proof ... 4				
Filled S......		2.00		3.25
Clear S.......		4.00		7.00
1980...... 7,414	...	...	...	.10
1980D..... 5,140	...	...	...	.10
1980S Proof ... 4		2.00		3.75
1981...... 7,492	...	...	...	.10
1981D..... 5,373	...	...	...	.10
1981S Proof ... 4		3.00		6.00
1982..........	...	...	...	.10
1982D..........	...	...	...	.10
1982S Proof		2.00		4.00

Values shown in these listings are averages of prices quoted by dealers throughout the country. The publisher of this book does not buy, sell, or appraise coins.

TWO CENT PIECES 1864-1873

The United States two cent piece was the first coin to use the motto "In God We Trust." The coins were never very popular and were soon discontinued. All were minted at Philadelphia. The few pieces coined in 1873 were for collecting purposes only and were not released for general circulation. The composition was the same as for the bronze cents of that period. Varieties of the 1864 coins have either large or small letters in the motto.

TWO CENTS OF 1864

Small Motto   Large Motto

Details explain the differences in these two well-known varieties. On the obverse, D in God is narrow on the large motto. The stem to the leaf shows plainly on the small motto variety. There is no stem on the large motto coin. First T in TRUST, small motto variety, is closer to ribbon crease at left.

GOOD—*At least IN GOD visible.*
V. GOOD—*WE weakly visible.*
FINE—*Complete motto visible. WE weak.*

Date	Thousands Minted	Avg. Dealers Pay		Average Retail Prices		
		Good	V. Good	Good	V. Good	Fine
1864 sm.	19,847	$25.00	$35.00	$45.00	$60.00	$80.00
1864 lg.		3.00	3.75	5.25	6.50	8.75
1865	13,640	3.00	3.75	5.25	6.50	8.75
1866	3,177	3.00	4.00	5.25	6.50	8.75
1867	2,939	3.00	4.00	5.25	6.50	8.75
1868	2,804	3.00	4.00	5.25	6.50	8.75
1869	1,546	3.25	4.50	5.50	6.75	10.00
1870	861	4.00	5.00	6.50	8.00	12.00
1871	721	5.00	7.00	7.50	9.00	13.00
1872	65	25.00	33.00	45.00	60.00	80.00
1873		Rare				

SILVER THREE CENT PIECES 1851-1873

All of the silver three cent pieces were coined at the Philadelphia Mint, with the exception of some made in 1851 at New Orleans. These have the mint mark O in the right field on the reverse.

The original weight of this piece was 12.375 grains, fineness .750. This was changed in 1853 to 11.52 grains, .900 fineness. The change was indicated by the addition of a wreath and a bundle of arrows on the reverse of those coins made after 1853. The star design was modified on two different occasions. These coins have a plain edge. They were originally issued to facilitate postal transactions, but were very unpopular because of their small size.

Pieces dated 1863 through 1873 were mostly exported or melted, with the exception of a few proof specimens made for collectors.

mint mark
o

GOOD—*Star worn smooth. Legend and date readable.*
VERY GOOD—*Outline of shield defined. Legend and date clear.*
FINE—*Only star points worn smooth.*

Variety 1 — No outline around star

Date	Thousands Minted	Avg. Dealers Pay Good	V. Good	Average Retail Prices Good	V. Good	Fine
1851	5,447	$4.50	$6.50	$9.00	$12.00	$15.00
1851O	720	6.25	9.00	12.25	18.50	27.50
1852	18,663	4.25	6.00	9.00	11.00	14.00
1853	11,400	4.25	6.00	9.00	11.00	14.00

Variety 2 — Three outlines to star, large date

1854	671	6.50	8.00	13.50	17.50	24.00
1855	139	9.00	12.00	16.00	22.00	32.00
1856	1,458	6.25	7.50	11.00	16.00	22.00
1857	1,042	6.25	7.50	11.00	16.00	22.00
1858	1,604	6.25	7.50	11.00	16.00	22.00

Variety 3 — Two outlines to star, small date

1859	365	6.25	7.50	11.00	15.00	21.00
1860	287	6.25	7.50	11.00	15.00	21.00
1861	498	6.25	7.50	11.00	15.00	21.00
1862	343	6.25	7.50	11.00	15.00	21.00
1863 thru 1873		Rare				

NICKEL THREE CENT PIECES 1865-1889

The three cent pieces struck in nickel were designed to replace the silver three cent coins. Composition is 75% copper and 25% nickel. All were coined at Philadelphia and have plain edges. The only major variety in this series occurs in the 1887, some of which show the date engraved over 1886. In 1877, 1878, and 1886 a limited number of pieces were struck for collecting purposes only. Various other dates were issued in small quantities, but these do not command high premiums, due to a general lack of interest in the series.

GOOD—Date and legends complete though III worn smooth.
V. GOOD—III is half worn. Rims complete.
FINE—Hair curls well defined.

Date	Thousands Minted	Avg. Dealers Pay Good	V. Good	Average Retail Prices Good	V. Good	Fine
1865	11,382	$3.00	$3.50	$5.00	$6.00	$7.50
1866	4,801	3.00	3.50	5.00	6.00	7.50
1867	3,915	3.00	3.50	5.00	6.00	7.50
1868	3,252	3.00	3.50	5.00	6.00	7.50
1869	1,604	3.00	3.50	5.00	6.00	7.50
1870	1,335	3.00	3.50	6.00	7.00	8.50
1871	604	3.25	4.00	6.00	7.50	9.00
1872	862	3.25	4.00	6.00	7.50	9.00
1873	1,173	3.00	3.50	6.00	7.50	9.00
1874	790	3.25	4.00	6.50	7.50	9.50
1875	228	4.25	5.25	8.50	10.00	12.00
1876	162	4.25	5.25	8.50	10.00	12.00
1877		Rare				
1878	2	Rare				
1879	41	17.50	20.00	35.00	40.00	45.00
1880	25	20.00	22.00	40.00	45.00	55.00
1881	1,081	3.00	3.50	5.00	6.00	8.00
1882	25	20.00	22.00	35.00	40.00	50.00
1883	11	24.00	27.00	50.00	55.00	75.00
1884	6	26.00	33.00	55.00	62.50	80.00
1885	5	30.00	40.00	60.00	70.00	100.00
1886	4	Rare				
1887	8	30.00	40.00	55.00	60.00	75.00
1888	41	16.00	20.00	30.00	35.00	40.00
1889	22	16.00	20.00	35.00	40.00	50.00

NICKEL FIVE CENT PIECES
Shield Type 1866-1883

The nickel five cent pieces were authorized by the Act of May 16, 1866. They were intended to retire fractional currency notes and replace the silver half dimes. The composition is 75% copper and 25% nickel. All were made at the mint in Philadelphia. A major variety with rays through the stars on the reverse was made in 1866 and part of 1867. Minor varieties exist, some of which are worth an additional premium.

Proofs dated 1877 and 1878 were struck for collectors.

Rays   Without Rays

GOOD—*All letters in motto readable.*
V. GOOD—*Motto stands out clearly. Rims worn slightly but even. Part of shield lines visible.*
FINE—*Half of each olive leaf is smooth.*

Variety 1 — Rays between stars 1866-1867

Date	Thousands Minted	Avg. Dealers Pay Good	V. Good	Average Retail Prices Good	V. Good	Fine
1866	14,742	$6.00	$ 8.00	$11.25	$14.00	$20.00
1867	30,909	7.00	9.50	13.50	18.00	29.00

Variety 2 — Without rays 1867-1883

Date	Thousands Minted	Good	V. Good	Good	V. Good	Fine
1867	inc. above	4.25	5.00	8.00	9.50	12.00
1868	28,817	4.25	5.00	8.00	9.50	12.00
1869	16,395	4.25	5.00	8.00	9.50	12.00
1870	4,806	5.00	6.00	8.50	10.50	13.00
1871	561	17.00	21.00	32.50	40.00	52.50
1872	6,036	5.00	6.00	8.50	10.50	13.00
1873	4,550	5.00	6.00	8.50	10.50	13.00
1874	3,538	5.50	6.50	10.00	12.00	15.00
1875	2,097	7.50	9.00	13.00	15.00	22.00
1876	2,530	7.00	8.00	13.00	15.00	22.00
1877		Rare				
1878		Rare				
1879	29	75.00	100.00	100.00	125.00	150.00
1880	20	90.00	110.00	125.00	150.00	175.00
1881	72	60.00	85.00	80.00	110.00	135.00
1882	11,477	4.25	5.00	8.00	9.50	12.00
1883	1,457	4.25	5.00	8.00	9.50	12.00

NICKEL FIVE CENT PIECES
Liberty Head Type 1883-1913

The composition of the nickel remained unchanged for the Liberty Head or "V" type pieces, all of which were coined at the Philadelphia Mint until 1912. In that year they were made additionally at the Denver and San Francisco mints. The branch mint coins have a small mint mark beneath the dot to the left of the word CENTS on the reverse.

The first issue of 1883 did not indicate the denomination. The word CENTS was added later that year and was retained until the end of the series.

GOOD—No detail in head. LIBERTY obliterated.
V. GOOD—At least 3 letters in LIBERTY readable.
FINE—All letters in LIBERTY show.

Variety 1 — Without CENTS 1883

Date	Millions Minted	Avg. Dealers Pay		Average Retail Prices		
		Good	V. Good	Good	V. Good	Fine
1883	5	$1.00	$1.50	$2.00	$3.00	$4.00

Variety 2 — With CENTS 1883-1913

1883	16	3.00	4.00	5.50	8.00	12.00
1884	11	3.00	4.00	6.00	8.25	13.00
1885	1	160.00	190.00	225.00	275.00	375.00

NICKEL FIVE CENT PIECES

Date	Millions Minted	Avg. Dealers Pay		Average Retail Prices		
		Good	V. Good	Good	V. Good	Fine
1886	3	$30.00	$37.00	$40.00	$60.00	$90.00
1887	15	1.65	2.00	3.50	5.00	15.00
1888	11	2.25	4.00	6.00	9.00	18.00
1889	16	1.50	2.50	3.50	5.00	14.00
1890	16	1.50	2.50	3.50	5.00	14.00
1891	17	1.50	2.00	3.50	5.00	14.00
1892	12	1.50	2.00	3.50	5.00	15.00
1893D	13	1.35	2.00	3.50	5.00	14.00
1894	5	2.50	3.50	5.50	8.00	17.00
1895	10	1.25	2.00	3.00	4.50	15.00
1896	9	1.25	2.00	3.50	5.00	15.00
1897	20	.40	.55	1.00	2.00	5.00
1898	12	.40	.55	1.00	2.00	5.00
1899	26	.40	.55	1.00	2.00	5.00
1900	27	.30	.50	.60	1.00	2.50
1901	26	.30	.50	.60	1.00	2.50
1902	31	.30	.50	.60	1.00	2.50
1903	28	.30	.50	.60	1.00	2.50
1904	21	.30	.50	.60	1.00	2.50
1905	30	.30	.50	.60	1.00	2.50
1906	39	.30	.50	.60	1.00	2.50
1907	39	.30	.50	.60	1.00	2.50
1908	23	.30	.50	.60	1.00	2.50
1909	12	.30	.60	.75	1.25	3.00
1910	30	.30	.50	.60	1.00	2.50
1911	40	.30	.50	.60	1.00	2.50

Location of mint mark.

1912	26	.30	.50	.60	1.00	2.25
1912D	8	.50	.75	1.35	2.00	5.50
1912S	0.2	25.00	36.00	35.00	50.00	65.00
1913					Unc. $200,000	

The famous 1913 Liberty Head nickel was not a regular mint issue. The reason for its existence has never been fully explained. Five specimens are known to exist, all of them in permanent collections.

NICKEL FIVE CENT PIECES
Indian Head or Buffalo Type 1913-1938

The Buffalo nickel was designed by James E. Fraser, whose initial F is below the date. He modeled the bison after Black Diamond in the New York Zoological Gardens. The three Indians used in the portrait were Irontail, Two Moons, and John Big Tree.

The first issue of 1913 has a buffalo standing on a mound inscribed FIVE CENTS, and beneath that a mint mark when warranted. Composition of 75% copper and 25% nickel, and weight 77.16 grains are the same as that of previous issues.

Interesting minor varieties in this series include the 1918D with 8 over 7 and the 1937D with one front leg of the buffalo missing. Coins with the date worn away have no premium value.

GOOD—Legends and date readable. Horn worn off.
V. GOOD—Half horn shows.
FINE—Three quarters of horn shows. Obv. rim intact.

Variety 1 — FIVE CENTS on mound 1913

Date	Millions Minted	Avg. Dealers Pay Good	V. Good	Average Retail Prices Good	V. Good	Fine
1913	31	$1.20	$1.40	$2.50	$3.25	$4.00
1913D	5	2.70	3.50	5.50	6.00	7.00
1913S	2	4.00	5.00	6.25	8.00	14.00

Mint mark below FIVE CENTS.

Variety 2 — FIVE CENTS recessed 1913-1938

1913	30	1.75	2.00	3.00	3.75	4.75
1913D	4	21.00	25.00	35.00	40.00	50.00
1913S	1	35.00	45.00	60.00	70.00	100.00

NICKEL FIVE CENT PIECES

Date	Millions Minted	Avg. Dealers Pay Good	V. Good	Average Retail Prices Good	V. Good	Fine
1914	21	$1.50	$2.00	$3.75	$4.50	$5.75
1914D	4	16.00	18.00	22.00	30.00	40.00
1914S	3	2.50	3.50	4.50	5.50	8.00
1915	21	.60	1.00	1.75	2.50	3.25
1915D	8	2.85	4.00	5.50	7.00	11.25
1915S	1	5.00	7.00	8.00	11.00	22.50
1916	63	.30	.45	.75	1.00	1.75
1916D	13	2.00	2.50	4.50	5.50	7.50
1916S	12	1.50	2.00	3.00	4.00	6.00
1917	51	.25	.50	.85	1.25	1.90
1917D	10	1.75	3.00	3.50	5.50	9.25
1917S	4	1.75	3.00	3.25	5.50	9.25
1918	32	.30	.50	.85	1.50	2.75
1918D 8 over 7		250.00	375.00	500.00	600.00	850.00
1918D	8	2.00	3.00	3.50	5.50	10.00
1918S	5	1.50	2.75	3.00	4.75	9.50

1918D, 8 over 7

1919	61	.30	.40	.65	.85	1.50
1919D	8	1.75	3.50	3.75	6.00	12.00
1919S	7	1.50	3.00	2.50	4.50	9.50
1920	63	.25	.35	.65	.85	1.50
1920D	9	1.50	2.50	3.00	4.50	8.75
1920S	10	.90	1.75	1.75	2.75	6.25
1921	11	.35	.55	.85	1.25	3.00
1921S	1	7.00	9.00	9.25	15.00	30.00
1923	36	.20	.30	.45	.65	1.25
1923S	6	.65	1.20	1.50	2.50	5.50
1924	22	.15	.25	.45	.65	1.25
1924D	5	.80	1.25	2.25	3.00	7.75
1924S	1	2.00	3.25	4.50	6.50	14.50
1925	35	.15	.25	.50	.70	1.25
1925D	4	1.50	3.00	3.50	5.50	11.00
1925S	6	1.10	2.25	2.25	4.00	6.75
1926	45	.10	.13	.40	.60	.95
1926D	6	1.00	1.75	2.00	3.75	9.00
1926S	1	2.75	4.25	5.50	8.50	15.50
1927	38	.07	.12	.40	.60	.95

NICKEL FIVE CENT PIECES

Date	Millions Minted	Avg. Dealers Pay		Average Retail Prices		
		Good	V. Good	Good	V. Good	Fine
1927D	6	$ .30	$ .65	$1.00	$1.75	$3.00
1927S	3	.45	.90	1.00	1.75	3.00
1928	23	.07	.12	.40	.60	.95
1928D	6	.15	.30	.75	1.00	2.25
1928S	7	.20	.35	.75	1.00	1.50
1929	36	.07	.12	.40	.50	.85
1929D	8	.15	.25	.60	.80	1.40
1929S	8	.15	.25	.55	.75	1.00
1930	23	.07	.12	.40	.50	.85
1930S	5	.20	.35	.50	.75	1.00
1931S	1	1.50	2.00	3.50	4.50	5.50
1934	20	.07	.10	.30	.45	.60
1934D	7	.10	.15	.45	.60	.85
1935	58	.07	.10	.30	.35	.45
1935D	12	.07	.10	.35	.45	.60
1935S	10	.07	.10	.35	.40	.50
1936	119	.07	.10	.30	.35	.40
1936D	25	.07	.10	.30	.40	.50
1936S	15	.07	.10	.30	.40	.50

1937D "3-Legged" Variety

1937	79	.07	.10	.30	.35	.45
1937D	18	.07	.10	.30	.40	.55
1937D Three-legged buffalo		100.00	175.00	175.00	200.00	235.00
1937S	6	.10	.15	.40	.45	.55
1938D	7	.07	.10	.40	.45	.55

Jefferson Type 1938 to Date

This coin design was selected in open competition. The initials of the winning artist, Felix Schlag, were added to the design in small letters beneath the bust starting in 1966. Coins were struck at all three mints. The mint mark is shown

NICKEL FIVE CENT PIECES

beside the date starting in 1968, and to the right of the building on the reverse of all earlier issues except those struck from 1942 thru 1945 in the wartime alloy. On these the mint mark appears as a large letter above the dome. Until 1979, this emergency issue was the only U.S. denomination on which the letter "P" (for the Philadelphia Mint) was ever used. Composition of the wartime alloy was 56% copper, 35% silver, and 9% manganese.

Mint mark at right of Monticello 1938-1942, 1946-1964

VERY GOOD—*Second porch pillar from right nearly gone, other three still visible but weak.*
FINE—*Cheekbone worn flat. Hairlines and eyebrow faint. Second pillar weak, especially at bottom.*
VERY FINE—*Second pillar plain and complete on both sides.*
EXTRA FINE—*Cheekbone, hairlines, eyebrow slightly worn but well defined. Base of triangle above pillars visible but weak.*

Variety 1 — 1938-1942

Date	Millions Minted	Avg. Dealers Pay V. Good	Fine	Average Retail Prices V. Good	Fine	V. Fine
1938	19	$ .07	$ .10	$ .15	$ .25	$ .40
1938D	5	.50	.90	1.10	1.45	1.65
1938S	4	1.00	1.50	2.00	2.25	3.00
1939	121	.06	.07	.15	.25	.35
1939D	3	2.40	3.50	4.00	4.50	5.50
1939S	7	.35	.60	.70	.90	1.25
1940	176	...	...	...	...	.20
1940D	44	...	...	...	...	.25
1940S	40	...	...	...	...	.30
1941	203	...	...	...	...	.15
1941D	53	...	...	...	...	.20
1941S	43	...	...	...	...	.25
1942	50	...	...	...	...	.25
1942D	14	.10	.20	.40	.75	1.00

NICKEL FIVE CENT PIECES
Variety 2 — Wartime alloy 1942-1945

Mint mark above Monticello 1942-1945

Date	Millions Minted	Avg. Dealers Pay		Average Retail Prices		
		V. Good	Fine	V. Good	Fine	V. Fine
1942P	58	$.40	$.40	$.50	$.50	.80
1942S	33	.40	.40	.50	.50	.70
1943P	271	.40	.40	.50	.50	.70
1943D	15	.40	.40	.50	.50	.70
1943S	104	.40	.40	.50	.50	.70
1944P	119	.40	.40	.50	.50	.70
1944D	32	.40	.40	.50	.50	.70
1944S	22	.40	.40	.50	.50	.70
1945P	119	.40	.40	.50	.50	.70
1945D	37	.40	.40	.50	.50	.70
1945S	59	.40	.40	.50	.50	.70

Variety 1 resumed 1946-1965

Date	Millions Minted	Avg. Dealers Pay		Average Retail Prices		
		V. Fine	Ex. Fine	V. Fine	Ex. Fine	Unc.
1946	161	...	...	...	.20	.60
1946D	45	...	...	.20	.30	.75
1946S	14	...	.15	.30	.45	1.25
1947	95	...	...	...	.20	.35
1947D	38	...	...	...	.25	1.00
1947S	25	...	.10	.25	.40	1.75
1948	89	...	...	...	.20	.50
1948D	45	...	.08	.25	.50	1.50
1948S	11	...	.15	.30	.50	2.00
1949	61	...	...	.15	.25	.75
1949D	36	...	...	.20	.35	1.50
1949S	10	...	.15	.40	.75	3.00
1950	10	...	.20	.40	.70	2.25
1950D	3	5.00	5.75	8.00	9.00	12.00
1951	29	...	...	.20	.30	1.00
1951D	20	...	...	.20	.30	2.00
1951S	8	.10	.45	.50	.90	3.00
1952	64	...	...	...	.20	.50
1952D	31	...	.08	.30	.65	2.25
1952S	21	...	.08	.20	.30	.85

NICKEL FIVE CENT PIECES

Date	Millions Minted	Avg. Dealers Pay V. Fine	Ex. Fine	Average Retail Prices V. Fine	Ex. Fine	Unc.
1953	47	...	...	...	$ .20	$ .30
1953D	60	...	...	...	.20	.50
1953S	19	...	$ .08	$ .20	.30	.55
1954	48	...	...	...	.15	.25
1954D	117	...	...	...	.15	.25
1954S	29	...	...	.15	.20	.30
1955	8	$ .10	.30	.50	.60	1.50
1955D	74	...	...	...	.15	.25
1956	36	...	...	...	.15	.25
1956D	67	...	...	...	.15	.25
1957	40	...	...	...	.15	.25
1957D	137	...	...	...	.15	.20
1958	18	...	.10	.15	.20	.35
1958D	168	...	...	...	.15	.20
1959	28	...	...	...	.15	.30
1959D	161	...	...	...	...	.15
1960	57	...	...	...	...	.15
1960D	193	...	...	...	...	.15
1961	77	...	...	...	...	.15
1961D	229	...	...	...	...	.15
1962	101	...	...	...	...	.15
1962D	280	...	...	...	...	.15
1963	179	...	...	...	...	.10
1963D	277	...	...	...	...	.10
1964	1,029	...	...	...	...	.10
1964D	1,787	...	...	...	...	.10
1965	136	...	...	...	...	.10

Location of mint mark starting with 1968

Variety 3 — Initials FS added 1966-

Date	Millions Minted					
1966	156	...	...	...	...	.10
1967	107	...	...	...	...	.10
1968D	91	...	...	...	...	.10
1968S	103	...	...	...	...	.10
1969D	203	...	...	...	...	.10
1969S	123	...	...	...	...	.10
1970D	515	...	...	...	...	.10
1970S	241	...	...	...	...	.10
1971	107	...	...	...	...	.70
1971D	316	...	...	...	...	.10
1971S Proof	3	...	.75	...	...	1.75

NICKEL FIVE CENT PIECES

Date	Millions Minted	Avg. Dealers Pay Ex. Fine	Proof	Average Retail Prices V. Fine	Ex. Fine	Unc.
1972	202	...	...	...	...	$ .10
1972D	352	...	...	...	...	.10
1972S Proof	3		$ .75			1.70
1973	384	...	...	...	...	.10
1973D	260	...	...	...	...	.10
1973S Proof	3		.75			2.50
1974	602	...	...	...	...	.10
1974D	277	...	...	...	...	.10
1974S Proof	3		1.60			4.00
1975	182	...	...	...	...	.10
1975D	402	...	...	...	...	.10
1975S Proof	3		1.00			3.00
1976	367	...	...	...	...	.10
1976D	563	...	...	...	...	.10
1976S Proof	4		.75			1.75
1977	585	...	...	...	...	.10
1977D	297	...	...	...	...	.10
1977S Proof	3		.75			1.50
1978	391	...	...	...	...	.10
1978D	313	...	...	...	...	.10
1978S Proof	3		.75			1.50
1979	463	...	...	...	...	.10
1979D	326	...	...	...	...	.10
1979S Proof	4					
Filled S			.75			1.50
Clear S			4.00			7.00
1980P	593	...	...	...	...	.10
1980D	502	...	...	...	...	.10
1980S Proof	4		.75			1.25
1981P	658	...	...	...	...	.10
1981D	365	...	...	...	...	.10
1981S Proof	4		.50			1.00
1982P		...	...	...	...	.10
1982D		...	...	...	...	.10
1982S Proof			.50			1.00

Values shown in these listings are averages of prices quoted by dealers throughout the country. The publisher of this book does not buy, sell, or appraise coins.

SILVER HALF DIMES 1794-1873

The 1792 Half Disme (dime) was the first authorized United States coinage, although silver pieces for general circulation were not minted until 1794. All of the early half dimes are very scarce; the bust type from 1829-1837 is less so, and the Liberty Seated type is the most common.

All were struck at Philadelphia until 1838, when coinage was also undertaken at New Orleans. Beginning in 1863, the San Francisco Mint coined this denomination. Mint marks are located on the reverse, either within or below the wreath; the edge is reeded. Many minor varieties exist.

Early half dimes weighed 20.8 grains of .892 fine silver. This was changed in 1837 to 20.625 grains of .900 fine silver. In 1853 the weight was again changed to 19.2 grains and arrows were placed beside the date to indicate this. The arrows were removed after 1855.

Half Disme 1792

FAIR—Details clear enough to identify.
GOOD—Eagle, wreath, bust outlined but lack details.
V. GOOD—Some details remain on face. All lettering readable.

Date	Thousands Minted	Avg. Dealers Pay Fair	Good		Average Retail Prices Fair	Good	V. Good
1792	2	$325.00	$650.00		$700.00	$1,200	$1,600

Small Eagle Reverse 1794-1797

        1794-1795   1796-1797

Date	Minted	Fair	Good		Fair	Good	V. Good
1794	86	200.00	500.00		400.00	800.00	1,000
1795	incl. above	175.00	450.00		350.00	700.00	900.00
1796	10	200.00	500.00		400.00	750.00	1,000
1797	44	175.00	450.00		350.00	650.00	900.00

SILVER HALF DIMES
Draped Bust, Large Eagle Reverse 1800-1805

FAIR—Details clear enough to identify.
GOOD—Date, stars, LIBERTY readable.
  Bust outlined but no details.
V. GOOD—Some details show.

Date	Thousands Minted	Avg. Dealers Pay Fair	Good	Average Retail Prices Fair	Good	V. Good
1800	24	$135.00	$300.00	$200.00	$400.00	$650.00
1801	34	150.00	310.00	210.00	410.00	675.00
1802	13	1,000	2,200	2,100	4,000	5,500
1803	38	135.00	300.00	200.00	400.00	650.00
1805	16	160.00	350.00	250.00	450.00	700.00

Liberty Cap Type 1829-1837

GOOD—Bust outlined, no detail. Date and legend readable.
V. GOOD—Complete legend and date plain. At least 3 letters of LIBERTY show clearly.
FINE—All letters in LIBERTY show.

Date	Thousands Minted	Avg. Dealers Pay Good	V. Good	Average Retail Prices Good	V. Good	Fine
1829	1,230	10.00	13.00	17.00	20.00	25.00
1830	1,240	10.00	13.00	17.00	20.00	25.00
1831	1,243	10.00	13.00	17.00	20.00	25.00
1832	965	10.00	13.00	17.00	20.00	25.00
1833	1,370	10.00	13.00	17.00	20.00	25.00
1834	1,480	10.00	13.00	17.00	20.00	25.00
1835	2,760	10.00	13.00	17.00	20.00	25.00
1836	1,900	10.00	13.00	17.00	20.00	25.00
1837	2,276	10.00	13.00	17.00	20.00	25.00

Liberty Seated Type 1837-1873
Variety 1 — No stars on obverse 1837-1838

GOOD—LIBERTY on shield smooth. Date and letters readable.
V. GOOD—At least 3 letters in LIBERTY are visible.
FINE—Entire LIBERTY visible, weak spots.

1837	2,276	20.00	27.50	47.50	60.00	80.00
1838O	70	27.50	40.00	44.00	55.00	75.00

SILVER HALF DIMES

Variety 2 — Stars on obverse 1838-1853

Date	Thousands Minted	Avg. Dealers Pay Good	V. Good	Average Retail Prices Good	V. Good	Fine
1838	2,255	$3.35	$4.00	$7.00	$8.25	$13.00
1839	1,069	3.35	4.00	7.00	8.25	13.00
1839O	1,034	4.50	6.00	9.00	12.50	17.50
1840	1,344	3.50	4.25	7.00	8.00	12.00
1840O	935	4.25	6.00	7.50	11.00	17.50
1841	1,150	3.35	4.25	7.00	8.00	12.00
1841O	815	4.50	8.00	12.00	17.00	25.00
1842	815	3.50	4.50	7.00	8.00	12.00
1842O	350	6.00	9.00	15.00	20.00	35.00
1843	1,165	3.35	4.25	7.00	8.00	12.00
1844	430	4.00	5.00	7.00	8.00	12.00
1844O	220	10.00	20.00	35.00	50.00	85.00
1845	1,564	3.35	4.00	7.00	8.00	12.00
1846	27	35.00	75.00	100.00	150.00	200.00
1847	1,274	3.35	4.00	7.00	8.00	12.00
1848	668	3.35	4.00	7.00	8.00	12.00
1848O	600	4.50	7.00	12.00	20.00	27.50
1849	1,309	3.35	4.00	7.00	8.00	12.00
1849O	140	15.00	23.00	25.00	40.00	65.00
1850	955	3.35	4.00	7.00	8.00	12.00
1850O	690	4.50	7.00	12.00	20.00	27.50
1851	781	3.35	4.00	7.00	8.00	12.00
1851O	860	4.50	8.00	12.00	17.00	25.00
1852	1,000	3.35	4.00	7.00	8.00	12.00
1852O	260	8.00	15.00	25.00	33.00	50.00
1853	135	7.50	10.00	14.00	24.00	37.50
1853O	160	50.00	60.00	100.00	125.00	200.00

Variety 3 — Arrows at date 1853-1855

1853	13,210	3.25	4.25	6.00	7.50	9.50
1853O	2,200	3.25	4.25	6.00	7.50	9.50
1854	5,740	3.25	4.25	6.00	7.50	9.50
1854O	1,560	3.25	4.25	7.00	8.50	11.00
1855	1,750	3.25	4.25	6.00	7.50	9.50
1855O	600	4.00	5.00	9.50	12.50	17.50

SILVER HALF DIMES
Variety 2 resumed 1856-1859

Date	Thousands Minted	Avg. Dealers Pay Good	V. Good	Average Retail Prices Good	V. Good	Fine
1856	4,880	$3.25	$4.25	$6.00	$8.00	$10.00
1856O	1,100	3.25	4.25	6.50	8.50	11.00
1857	7,280	3.25	4.25	6.00	8.00	10.00
1857O	1,380	3.25	4.25	6.50	8.50	11.00
1858	3,500	3.25	4.25	6.00	8.00	10.00
1858O	1,660	3.25	4.25	6.50	8.50	11.00
1859	340	5.00	8.00	10.00	17.50	25.00
1859O	560	5.00	8.00	10.00	17.50	22.50

Variety 4 — Legend on obverse 1860-1873

Mint mark below bow 1860-1869, 1872-1873.

Mint mark above bow 1871-1872.

1860	799	3.25	4.00	5.50	6.50	9.00
1860O	1,060	3.25	4.00	5.50	6.50	10.00
1861	3,361	3.25	4.00	5.25	6.50	8.00
1862	1,493	3.25	4.00	5.25	6.50	8.00
1863	18	25.00	32.00	55.00	65.00	90.00
1863S	100	8.00	10.00	14.00	17.50	22.50
1864	48	75.00	100.00	150.00	190.00	220.00
1864S	90	9.00	12.00	22.50	30.00	45.00
1865	13	30.00	40.00	75.00	90.00	125.00
1865S	120	5.50	7.00	12.50	17.50	25.00
1866	11	30.00	40.00	75.00	100.00	125.00
1866S	120	5.50	7.00	12.50	17.50	22.50
1867	9	35.00	50.00	115.00	165.00	215.00
1867S	120	5.50	7.00	12.50	17.50	22.50
1868	89	6.50	9.00	20.00	30.00	40.00
1868S	280	3.25	4.00	7.50	10.00	15.00
1869	209	3.25	4.00	7.00	9.00	12.00
1869S	230	3.25	4.00	7.50	10.00	15.00
1870	537	3.25	4.00	5.50	8.00	10.00
1870S	Unique					
1871	1,874	3.25	4.00	5.50	8.00	10.00
1871S	161	6.50	10.00	16.00	23.00	35.00
1872	2,948	3.25	4.00	5.50	8.00	10.00
1872S	837	3.25	5.00	6.00	10.00	16.00
1873	713	3.25	4.00	5.50	8.00	10.00
1873S	324	3.25	5.00	6.00	10.00	16.00

DIMES

The design of the early dimes was similar to that of the half dimes; the weight was exactly double and the alloy the same. All dimes have a reeded edge. Those coins before 1809 do not show the denomination. All of the early dates are rare, but there are many common dates in the Liberty Seated series. Several interesting overdates and varieties are known, some of them worth an additional premium.

Most of the dimes dated 1853-1855 and 1873-1874 have arrows at the date to indicate a change in weight. All dimes coined after 1874 weigh 38.58 grains of .900 fine silver. Mint marks are the same as for half dimes, but additional pieces were coined at the Carson City Mint from 1871 through 1878.

Draped Bust, Small Eagle Reverse 1796-1797

FAIR—Details clear enough to identify.
GOOD—Date readable. Bust outlined, but no detail.
V. GOOD—All but deepest drapery folds worn smooth. Hairlines nearly gone and curls lack detail.

Date	Thousands Minted	Avg. Dealers Pay		Average Retail Prices		
		Fair	Good	Fair	Good	V. Good
1796	22	$250.00	$600.00	$600.00	$900.00	$1,750
1797	25	200.00	550.00	550.00	850.00	1,600

Draped Bust, Heraldic Eagle Reverse 1798-1807

1798	28	125.00	300.00	175.00	375.00	750.00
1800	22	100.00	250.00	175.00	350.00	700.00
1801	35	100.00	250.00	175.00	350.00	700.00
1802	11	100.00	250.00	175.00	350.00	700.00
1803	33	100.00	250.00	175.00	350.00	700.00
1804	8	250.00	400.00	325.00	600.00	950.00
1805	121	85.00	225.00	175.00	350.00	700.00
1807	165	85.00	225.00	175.00	350.00	700.00

DIMES
Capped Bust Type 1809-1837

GOOD—Date, letters and stars discernible. Bust outlined, no details.
V. GOOD—Legends and date plain. Minimum of 3 letters in LIBERTY show.
FINE—Full LIBERTY. Ear and shoulder clasp visible. Part of rim shows on both sides.

Date	Thousands Minted	Avg. Dealers Pay Good	V. Good	Average Retail Prices Good	V. Good	Fine
1809	51	$35.00	$65.00	$80.00	$135.00	$190.00
1811	65	25.00	30.00	50.00	75.00	100.00
1814	421	13.00	16.00	30.00	36.00	50.00
1820	943	12.00	15.00	25.00	35.00	45.00
1821	1,187	12.00	15.00	25.00	35.00	45.00
1822	100	32.00	45.00	65.00	100.00	185.00
1823	440	12.00	15.00	25.00	35.00	45.00
1824		15.00	18.00	30.00	40.00	60.00
1825	510	13.00	16.00	25.00	35.00	45.00
1827	1,215	12.00	15.00	22.50	30.00	40.00
1828	125	12.00	16.00	30.00	37.50	50.00
1829	770	9.50	12.50	16.00	22.50	30.00
1830	510	8.75	11.50	16.00	22.50	30.00
1831	771	8.75	11.50	16.00	22.50	30.00
1832	522	8.75	11.50	16.00	22.50	30.00
1833	485	8.75	11.50	16.00	22.50	30.00
1834	635	8.75	11.50	16.00	22.50	30.00
1835	1,410	8.75	11.50	16.00	22.50	30.00
1836	1,190	8.75	11.50	16.00	22.50	30.00
1837	360	8.75	11.50	16.00	22.50	30.00

Liberty Seated Type 1837-1891

GOOD—LIBERTY on shield smooth. Date and letters readable.
V. GOOD—At least 3 letters in LIBERTY are visible.
FINE—Entire LIBERTY visible, weak spots.

Variety 1 — No stars on obverse 1837-1838

1837	682	19.00	25.00	35.00	50.00	75.00
1838O	406	22.50	32.50	40.00	65.00	100.00

DIMES

Variety 2 — Stars on obverse 1838-1853

Date	Thousands Minted	Avg. Dealers Pay Good	V. Good	Average Retail Prices Good	V. Good	Fine
1838	1,992	$3.50	$4.50	$8.00	$10.00	$12.50
1839	1,053	3.50	4.00	5.50	6.00	10.00
1839O	1,323	3.50	4.50	6.50	8.00	14.00
1840	1,359	3.00	5.00	5.50	6.00	10.00
1840O	1,175	3.50	4.50	7.00	8.00	15.00
1841	1,622	2.25	3.25	4.75	5.50	9.00
1841O	2,007	2.75	4.00	7.00	10.00	15.00
1842	1,887	2.25	3.25	4.75	5.50	9.00
1842O	2,020	2.50	3.50	4.75	6.00	10.00
1843	1,370	2.25	3.25	4.75	5.50	9.00
1843O	150	14.00	19.00	30.00	50.00	80.00
1844	72	16.00	25.00	30.00	50.00	80.00
1845	1,755	2.25	3.25	4.75	5.50	9.00
1845O	230	5.00	8.50	15.00	25.00	40.00
1846	31	25.00	35.00	45.00	55.00	90.00
1847	245	3.50	5.00	10.00	14.00	30.00
1848	451	2.50	3.50	5.00	6.50	11.00
1849	839	2.25	3.25	4.75	6.00	9.00
1849O	300	4.50	7.00	10.00	12.00	20.00
1850	1,931	2.25	3.25	4.75	5.50	9.00
1850O	510	3.50	5.00	8.00	10.00	15.00
1851	1,026	2.25	3.25	4.75	5.50	9.00
1851O	400	3.50	5.00	8.00	10.00	15.00
1852	1,535	2.25	3.25	4.75	5.50	9.00
1852O	430	3.50	5.00	8.00	10.00	15.00
1853	95	12.00	15.00	25.00	30.00	45.00

Variety 3 — Arrows at date 1853-1855

Date	Thousands Minted	Good	V. Good	Good	V. Good	Fine
1853	12,078	2.75	3.75	6.00	8.00	11.00
1853O	1,100	3.25	4.25	7.00	9.00	15.00
1854	4,470	2.75	3.75	6.00	8.00	12.00
1854O	1,770	3.25	4.25	7.00	9.00	15.00
1855	2,075	2.75	3.75	6.00	8.00	12.00

DIMES

Variety 2 resumed 1856-1860

Date	Thousands Minted	Avg. Dealers Pay		Average Retail Prices		
		Good	V. Good	Good	V. Good	Fine
1856	5,780	$2.25	$3.25	$4.25	$6.00	$12.00
1856O	1,180	2.25	3.50	4.25	6.00	12.00
1856S	70	16.50	25.00	35.00	55.00	80.00
1857	5,580	2.25	3.25	4.00	5.00	7.50
1857O	1,540	2.25	3.25	4.00	5.00	7.75
1858	1,540	2.25	3.25	4.00	5.00	7.50
1858O	290	3.00	6.00	8.00	15.00	25.00
1858S	60	13.00	25.00	30.00	55.00	90.00
1859	430	2.25	3.25	5.00	6.50	9.00
1859O	480	2.25	3.25	5.00	6.50	9.00
1859S	60	12.00	20.00	30.00	40.00	70.00
1860S	140	5.00	7.50	10.00	15.00	30.00

Variety 4 — Legend on obverse 1860-1873

Date	Thousands Minted	Avg. Dealers Pay		Average Retail Prices		
		Good	V. Good	Good	V. Good	Fine
1860	607	2.25	3.25	4.00	5.00	7.50
1860O	40	150.00	250.00	325.00	385.00	700.00
1861	1,884	2.25	3.25	4.00	5.00	7.50
1861S	172	8.00	11.00	15.00	22.00	35.00
1862	848	2.25	3.25	4.00	5.00	7.50
1862S	181	5.00	7.50	15.00	20.00	30.00
1863	14	32.00	45.00	75.00	100.00	135.00
1863S	157	5.00	9.00	18.00	23.00	40.00
1864	11	32.00	45.00	75.00	100.00	135.00
1864S	230	5.00	7.50	12.00	18.00	30.00
1865	10	37.50	50.00	75.00	110.00	150.00
1865S	175	5.00	7.50	12.00	18.00	30.00
1866	9	40.00	60.00	100.00	125.00	200.00
1866S	135	5.00	8.00	15.00	18.50	30.00
1867	7	55.00	75.00	160.00	190.00	275.00
1867S	140	5.00	8.00	12.50	16.00	27.50
1868	465	2.25	3.25	5.00	6.50	10.00
1868S	260	3.75	4.75	10.00	12.50	20.00
1869	257	2.25	3.25	5.00	6.50	10.00
1869S	450	3.50	4.50	8.00	10.00	15.00
1870	471	2.25	3.25	4.00	5.00	7.50
1870S	50	22.50	32.50	50.00	65.00	110.00
1871	908	2.25	3.25	4.00	5.00	7.50
1871CC	20	90.00	130.00	250.00	350.00	700.00
1871S	320	5.00	8.00	11.00	19.00	30.00

DIMES

Date	Thousands Minted	Avg. Dealers Pay Good	V. Good	Average Retail Prices Good	V. Good	Fine
1872	2,396	$2.25	$3.25	$4.00	$5.00	$7.50
1872CC	35	55.00	75.00	140.00	175.00	375.00
1872S	190	5.50	8.00	13.00	17.50	30.00
1873	1,569	2.25	3.25	4.00	5.00	7.50
1873CC	12	Unique				

Variety 5 — Arrows at date 1873-1874

Date	Thousands Minted	Good	V. Good	Good	V. Good	Fine
1873	2,378	5.50	7.50	11.00	15.00	27.50
1873CC	19	200.00	325.00	325.00	450.00	650.00
1873S	455	7.50	11.00	16.00	21.00	32.50
1874	2,941	5.50	7.50	11.00	15.00	27.50
1874CC	11	250.00	450.00	600.00	900.00	1,750
1874S	240	10.00	16.00	21.00	35.00	60.00

Variety 4 resumed 1875-1891

Date	Thousands Minted	Good	V. Good	Good	V. Good	Fine
1875	10,351	2.00	2.75	4.00	4.50	6.50
1875CC	4,645	2.00	4.00	5.00	9.00	17.50
1875S	9,070	2.00	2.75	4.00	4.50	6.50
1876	11,461	2.00	2.75	4.00	4.50	6.50
1876CC	8,270	2.00	2.75	4.00	4.50	6.50
1876S	10,420	2.00	2.75	4.00	4.50	6.50
1877	7,311	2.00	2.75	4.00	4.50	6.50
1877CC	7,700	2.00	2.75	4.00	4.50	6.50
1877S	2,340	2.00	2.75	4.00	4.50	6.50
1878	1,679	2.00	2.75	4.00	4.50	6.50
1878CC	200	8.00	15.00	20.00	30.00	50.00
1879	15	28.00	35.00	40.00	50.00	70.00
1880	37	22.00	30.00	35.00	45.00	60.00
1881	25	24.00	32.00	37.50	47.50	65.00
1882	3,911	2.00	2.75	4.00	4.50	6.50
1883	7,676	2.00	2.75	4.00	4.50	6.50
1884	3,366	2.00	2.75	4.00	4.50	6.50
1884S	565	5.00	8.00	11.00	15.00	20.00
1885	2,533	2.00	2.75	4.00	4.50	6.50
1885S	44	40.00	60.00	90.00	120.00	170.00
1886	6,378	2.00	2.75	4.00	4.50	6.50
1886S	207	5.00	8.00	11.00	15.00	20.00
1887	11,284	2.00	2.75	4.00	4.50	6.50
1887S	4,454	2.00	2.75	4.00	4.50	6.50
1888	5,496	2.00	2.75	4.00	4.50	6.50
1888S	1,720	2.00	2.75	4.00	4.50	6.50
1889	7,381	2.00	2.75	4.00	4.50	6.50
1889S	973	4.50	6.50	11.00	15.00	20.00
1890	9,912	2.00	2.75	4.00	4.50	6.50
1890S	1,423	2.25	3.50	5.00	7.00	15.00
1891	15,311	2.00	2.75	4.00	4.50	6.50
1891O	4,540	2.00	2.75	4.00	4.50	6.50
1891S	3,196	2.00	2.75	4.00	4.50	6.50

DIMES

Barber or Liberty Head Type 1892-1916

This coin was designed by Charles E. Barber, who also engraved the similar 25c and 50c pieces. His initial B is on the truncation of the neck. Only 24 specimens of the rare 1894S dime were minted. Coins were struck at Philadelphia, New Orleans, San Francisco, and Denver. Mint marks are on the reverse, below the wreath. As a rule, these coins are collected only in fine or better condition.

GOOD—Date and letters plain. LIBERTY over brow is obliterated.
VERY GOOD—At least 3 letters visible in LIBERTY.
FINE—All letters in LIBERTY visible, though some are weak.

Date	Millions Minted	Avg. Dealers Pay Good	Fine	Average Retail Prices Good	V. Good	Fine
1892	12	*$1.00*	*$2.50*	*$1.25*	*$1.50*	$5.00
1892O	4	2.00	5.00	4.50	7.00	10.00
1892S	1	12.00	27.50	24.00	33.00	50.00
1893	3	1.75	5.00	6.00	7.50	12.00
1893O	2	4.50	12.00	12.00	15.00	27.50
1893S	2	3.25	7.00	7.50	9.00	14.00
1894	1	3.50	8.00	8.00	10.00	16.00
1894O	0.7	15.00	40.00	30.00	41.00	70.00
1894S		Rare				
1895	0.7	25.00	50.00	50.00	60.00	85.00
1895O	0.4	80.00	120.00	115.00	150.00	190.00
1895S	1	7.00	20.00	12.00	18.00	27.50
1896	2	3.00	9.00	6.00	9.00	16.00
1896O	0.6	25.00	50.00	40.00	45.00	75.00
1896S	0.6	17.00	40.00	35.00	45.00	70.00
1897	11	*1.00*	*1.25*	*1.25*	*1.50*	4.00
1897O	0.7	15.00	37.50	30.00	37.00	60.00
1897S	1	4.00	12.00	7.50	11.00	20.00
1898	16	*1.00*	*1.25*	*1.25*	*1.50*	4.00
1898O	2	2.25	7.00	4.00	6.50	14.00
1898S	2	2.00	6.00	4.00	6.00	10.00
1899	20	*1.00*	*1.25*	*1.25*	*1.50*	4.00
1899O	3	1.75	7.00	4.00	6.50	15.00
1899S	2	1.75	6.00	4.50	7.00	11.00
1900	18	*1.00*	*1.25*	*1.25*	*1.50*	4.00
1900O	2	2.00	7.00	5.00	7.00	15.00

DIMES

Date	Millions Minted	Avg. Dealers Pay Good	Fine	Average Retail Prices Good	V. Good	Fine
1900S	5	*$1.00*	$3.50	*$1.25*	$4.25	$6.00
1901	19	*1.00*	*1.25*	*1.25*	*1.50*	3.00
1901O	6	*1.00*	3.50	*1.25*	*1.50*	7.00
1901S	0.6	25.00	60.00	35.00	50.00	90.00
1902	21	*1.00*	*1.25*	*1.25*	*1.50*	3.00
1902O	4	*1.00*	3.50	*1.25*	*1.50*	7.00
1902S	2	1.75	6.00	3.25	7.00	12.00
1903	19	*1.00*	*1.25*	*1.25*	*1.50*	3.00
1903O	8	*1.00*	2.50	*1.25*	*1.50*	6.00
1903S	0.6	15.00	30.00	25.00	32.00	50.00
1904	15	*1.00*	*1.25*	*1.25*	*1.50*	3.00
1904S	0.8	12.00	22.00	16.00	21.00	35.00
1905	15	*1.00*	*1.25*	*1.25*	*1.50*	3.00
1905O	3	*1.00*	4.00	*1.25*	4.00	9.00
1905S	7	*1.00*	2.75	*1.25*	2.00	6.00
1906	20	*1.00*	*1.25*	*1.25*	*1.50*	3.00
1906D	4	*1.00*	2.75	*1.25*	2.00	6.00
1906O	3	*1.00*	6.00	*1.25*	6.00	12.00
1906S	3	*1.00*	3.25	*1.25*	*1.50*	5.00
1907	22	*1.00*	*1.25*	*1.25*	*1.50*	3.00
1907D	4	*1.00*	2.75	*1.25*	2.00	6.00
1907O	5	*1.00*	2.75	*1.25*	*1.50*	3.00
1907S	3	*1.00*	3.00	*1.25*	*1.50*	3.00
1908	11	*1.00*	*1.25*	*1.25*	*1.50*	3.00
1908D	7	*1.00*	*1.25*	*1.25*	*1.50*	3.00
1908O	2	1.50	5.00	3.25	6.00	10.00
1908S	3	*1.00*	2.75	*1.25*	*1.50*	6.00
1909	10	*1.00*	*1.25*	*1.25*	*1.50*	3.00
1909D	1	1.75	6.50	4.00	6.00	12.00
1909O	2	*1.00*	4.25	*1.25*	4.00	8.00
1909S	1	2.75	7.50	5.00	7.00	16.50
1910	11	*1.00*	*1.25*	*1.25*	*1.50*	3.00
1910D	3	*1.00*	1.50	*1.25*	*1.50*	3.00
1910S	1	*1.00*	4.00	*1.25*	5.50	9.00
1911	19	*1.00*	*1.25*	*1.25*	*1.50*	4.00
1911D	11	*1.00*	*1.25*	*1.25*	*1.50*	4.00
1911S	3	*1.00*	*1.25*	*1.25*	*1.50*	5.00
1912	19	*1.00*	*1.25*	*1.25*	*1.50*	4.00
1912D	12	*1.00*	*1.25*	*1.25*	*1.50*	4.00
1912S	3	*1.00*	2.25	*1.25*	*1.50*	5.50
1913	20	*1.00*	*1.25*	*1.25*	*1.50*	4.00
1913S	0.5	4.00	17.00	8.00	13.00	30.00
1914	17	*1.00*	*1.25*	*1.25*	*1.50*	4.00
1914D	12	*1.00*	*1.25*	*1.25*	*1.50*	4.00
1914S	2	*1.00*	2.25	*1.25*	*1.50*	5.50
1915	6	*1.00*	*1.25*	*1.25*	*1.50*	5.00
1915S	1	*1.00*	3.50	*1.25*	3.00	8.00
1916	18	*1.00*	*1.25*	*1.25*	*1.50*	4.00
1916S	6	*1.00*	*1.25*	*1.25*	*1.50*	4.00

DIMES

Winged Head of Liberty or "Mercury" Type
1916-1945

This series is very popular among collectors, as most dates are still plentiful. Rare varieties of 1942 have the date engraved over 1941. All coins of this type have a premium in uncirculated condition. The design is by A. A. Weinman, whose monogram appears above the date. Mint marks are found on the reverse at the lower left of the fasces. Later dates are normally found in better condition and are listed accordingly.

Location of mint mark.

GOOD—*Letters and dates clear. Lines and diagonal bands in fasces are obliterated.*
VERY GOOD—*One-third of sticks discernible in fasces.*
FINE—*All sticks in fasces are defined. Diagonal bands worn at center high points only.*
V. FINE—*Diagonal bands show where they cross fasces.*

Date	Millions Minted	Avg. Dealers Pay Good	Fine	Average Retail Prices Good	V. Good	Fine
1916	22	$.80	$1.00	$1.00	$1.25	$1.40
1916D	0.3	275.00	575.00	500.00	650.00	950.00
1916S	10	.80	1.50	1.00	1.40	4.75
1917	55	.80	1.00	1.00	1.25	1.40
1917D	9	.80	3.00	2.75	4.00	6.75
1917S	27	.80	1.30	1.00	1.25	1.40
1918	27	.80	1.00	1.00	1.25	1.40
1918D	23	.80	1.50	1.00	1.25	1.40
1918S	19	.80	1.30	1.00	1.25	1.40
1919	36	.80	1.00	1.00	1.25	1.40
1919D	10	.80	2.00	2.75	3.50	5.50
1919S	9	.80	2.00	2.75	3.50	5.50
1920	59	.80	1.00	1.00	1.25	1.40
1920D	19	.80	1.00	1.00	1.25	1.40
1920S	14	.80	1.00	1.00	1.25	1.40
1921	1	15.00	45.00	25.00	35.00	80.00
1921D	1	25.00	55.00	35.00	45.00	90.00
1923	50	.80	1.00	1.00	1.25	1.40

DIMES

Date	Millions Minted	Avg. Dealers Pay Good	Avg. Dealers Pay Fine	Average Retail Prices Good	Average Retail Prices V. Good	Average Retail Prices Fine
1923S	6	*$.80*	*$2.00*	*$1.00*	*$1.25*	*$1.40*
1924	24	*.80*	*.80*	*1.00*	*1.25*	*1.40*
1924D	7	*.80*	*.80*	*1.00*	*1.25*	*1.40*
1924S	7	*.80*	*.80*	*1.00*	*1.25*	*1.40*
1925	26	*.80*	*.80*	*1.00*	*1.25*	*1.40*
1925D	5	*.80*	*5.00*	*3.50*	*4.00*	*7.50*
1925S	6	*.80*	*.80*	*1.00*	*1.25*	*1.40*
1926	32	*.80*	*.80*	*1.00*	*1.25*	*1.40*
1926D	7	*.80*	*.80*	*1.00*	*1.25*	*1.40*
1926S	2	4.00	7.50	5.75	8.00	11.50
1927	28	*.80*	*.80*	*1.00*	*1.25*	*1.40*
1927D	5	*.80*	2.25	2.75	3.50	5.00
1927S	5	*.80*	*.80*	*1.00*	*1.25*	*1.40*
1928	19	*.80*	*.80*	*1.00*	*1.25*	*1.40*
1928D	4	*.80*	1.75	*1.00*	*1.25*	*1.40*
1928S	7	*.80*	*.80*	*1.00*	*1.25*	*1.40*
1929	26	*.80*	*.80*	*1.00*	*1.25*	*1.40*
1929D	5	*.80*	*.80*	*1.00*	*1.25*	*1.40*
1929S	5	*.80*	*.80*	*1.00*	*1.25*	*1.40*
1930	7	*.80*	*.80*	*1.00*	*1.25*	*1.40*
1930S	2	1.35	1.85	3.25	4.00	4.50
1931	3	*.80*	*.80*	*1.00*	*1.25*	*1.40*
1931D	1	3.00	4.75	6.50	7.50	9.00
1931S	2	1.50	2.65	3.25	4.00	4.50
1934	24	*.70*	*.70*	*1.00*	*1.00*	*1.25*
1934D	7	*.70*	*.70*	*1.00*	*1.00*	*1.25*
1935	59	*.70*	*.70*	*1.00*	*1.00*	*1.25*
1935D	10	*.70*	*.70*	*1.00*	*1.00*	*1.25*
1935S	16	*.70*	*.70*	*1.00*	*1.00*	*1.25*
1936	88	*.70*	*.70*	*1.00*	*1.00*	*1.25*
1936D	16	*.70*	*.70*	*1.00*	*1.00*	*1.25*
1936S	9	*.70*	*.70*	*1.00*	*1.00*	*1.25*
1937	57	*.70*	*.70*	*1.00*	*1.00*	*1.25*
1937D	14	*.70*	*.70*	*1.00*	*1.00*	*1.25*
1937S	10	*.70*	*.70*	*1.00*	*1.00*	*1.25*
1938	22	*.70*	*.70*	*1.00*	*1.00*	*1.25*
1938D	6	*.70*	*.70*	*1.00*	*1.00*	*1.25*
1938S	8	*.70*	*.70*	*1.00*	*1.00*	*1.25*
1939	68	*.70*	*.70*	*1.00*	*1.00*	*1.25*
1939D	24	*.70*	*.70*	*1.00*	*1.00*	*1.25*
1939S	11	*.70*	*.70*	*1.00*	*1.00*	*1.25*
1940	65	*.70*	*.70*	*1.00*	*1.00*	*1.25*
1940D	21	*.70*	*.70*	*1.00*	*1.00*	*1.25*
1940S	22	*.70*	*.70*	*1.00*	*1.00*	*1.25*
1941	175	*.70*	*.70*	*1.00*	*1.00*	*1.25*
1941D	46	*.70*	*.70*	*1.00*	*1.00*	*1.25*
1941S	43	*.70*	*.70*	*1.00*	*1.00*	*1.25*

DIMES

Date	Millions Minted	Avg. Dealers Pay V. Good	Fine	Average Retail Prices V. Good	Fine	V. Fine
1942	205	$.70	$.70	$1.00	$1.25	$1.40
1942, 2 over 1		210.00	250.00	350.00	375.00	400.00
1942D	61	.70	.70	1.00	1.25	1.40
1942D, 2 over 1		235.00	275.00	375.00	400.00	500.00
1942S	49	.70	.70	1.00	1.25	1.40
1943	192	.70	.70	1.00	1.25	1.40
1943D	72	.70	.70	1.00	1.25	1.40
1943S	60	.70	.70	1.00	1.25	1.40
1944	231	.70	.70	1.00	1.25	1.40
1944D	62	.70	.70	1.00	1.25	1.40
1944S	49	.70	.70	1.00	1.25	1.40
1945	159	.70	.70	1.00	1.25	1.40
1945D	40	.70	.70	1.00	1.25	1.40
1945S	42	.70	.70	1.00	1.25	1.40

Roosevelt Type 1946 to Date

The dime honoring President Franklin D. Roosevelt was designed by John R. Sinnock, whose initials are to the left of the date. The majority of these coins are common and worth a premium only for their silver content. Most coins in uncirculated condition have an additional premium.

Mint marks are on the reverse at the lower left of the torch on the silver pieces and above the date on the clad coins.

The clad coinage started in 1965 has a copper core and a layer of copper-nickel on each side. Those coined at San Francisco after 1967 were issued only as proofs and not for general circulation.

Mint mark on reverse 1946-1964.

FINE—*Torch flame smooth. Vertical lines in torch show, horizontal lines smooth.*
VERY FINE—*Hair above ear slightly worn. All vertical lines on torch plain.*
EXTRA FINE—*All lines of torch, flame and hair very plain.*

Date	Millions Minted	Avg. Dealers Pay Fine	V. Fine	Average Retail Prices Fine	V. Fine	Ex. Fine
1946	255	$.60	$.60	$.70	$.70	$.80
1946D	61	.60	.60	.70	.70	.80

DIMES

Date	Millions Minted	Avg. Dealers Pay Fine	V. Fine	Average Retail Prices Fine	V. Fine	Ex. Fine
1946S	28	*$.60*	*$.60*	*$.70*	*$.70*	*$.80*
1947	122	.60	.60	.70	.70	.80
1947D	47	.60	.60	.70	.70	.80
1947S	35	.60	.60	.70	.70	.80
1948	75	.60	.60	.70	.70	.80
1948D	53	.60	.60	.70	.70	.80
1948S	36	.60	.60	.70	.70	.80
1949	31	.60	.60	.70	.70	2.00
1949D	26	.60	.60	.70	.70	.80
1949S	14	.60	.60	.70	.70	2.00
1950	50	.60	.60	.70	.70	.80
1950D	47	.60	.60	.70	.70	.80
1950S	20	.60	.60	.70	.70	.80
1951	104	.60	.60	.70	.70	.80
1951D	57	.60	.60	.70	.70	.80
1951S	32	.60	.60	.70	.70	.80
1952	99	.60	.60	.70	.70	.80
1952D	122	.60	.60	.70	.70	.80
1952S	44	.60	.60	.70	.70	.80
1953	54	.60	.60	.70	.70	.80
1953D	136	.60	.60	.70	.70	.80
1953S	39	.60	.60	.70	.70	.80
1954	114	.60	.60	.70	.70	.80
1954D	106	.60	.60	.70	.70	.80
1954S	23	.60	.60	.70	.70	.80
1955	13	.60	.60	.70	.70	.80
1955D	14	.60	.60	.70	.70	.80
1955S	19	.60	.60	.70	.70	.80
1956	109	.60	.60	.70	.70	.80
1956D	108	.60	.60	.70	.70	.80
1957	161	.60	.60	.70	.70	.80
1957D	113	.60	.60	.70	.70	.80
1958	33	.60	.60	.70	.70	.80
1958D	137	.60	.60	.70	.70	.80
1959	87	.60	.60	.70	.70	.80
1959D	165	.60	.60	.70	.70	.80
1960	72	.60	.60	.70	.70	.80
1960D	200	.60	.60	.70	.70	.80
1961	97	.60	.60	.70	.70	.80
1961D	209	.60	.60	.70	.70	.80
1962	76	.60	.60	.70	.70	.80
1962D	335	.60	.60	.70	.70	.80
1963	127	.60	.60	.70	.70	.80
1963D	421	.60	.60	.70	.70	.80
1964	933	.60	.60	.70	.70	.80
1964D	1,358	.60	.60	.70	.70	.80

Common silver coins are worth a premium only for their silver content. This price may vary according to prevailing market value of silver bullion. See page 4 for details.

DIMES

Mint mark on obverse starting 1968.

Date	Millions Minted	Avg. Dealers Pay Ex. Fine	Proof	Average Retail Prices Ex. Fine	Unc.	Proof
1965	1,652	...		...	$ .20	
1966	1,383	...		...	.20	
1967	2,244	...		...	.20	
1968	424	...		...	.20	
1968D	481	...		...	.20	
1968S Proof	3		$ .50			$.85
1969	145	...		...	.50	
1969D	563	...		...	.20	
1969S Proof	3		.50			.85
1970	346	...		...	.20	
1970D	755	...		...	.20	
1970S Proof	3		.75			1.50
1971	163	...		...	.20	
1971D	378	...		...	.20	
1971S Proof	3		.50			.85
1972	432	...		...	.20	
1972D	330	...		...	.20	
1972S Proof	3		.50			.85
1973	316	...		...	.20	
1973D	455	...		...	.20	
1973S Proof	3		.80			1.75
1974	470	...		...	.20	
1974D	571	...		...	.20	
1974S Proof	3		.80			1.75
1975	586	...		...	.20	
1975D	314	...		...	.20	
1975S Proof	3		1.10			2.00
1976	568	...		...	.20	
1976D	695	...		...	.20	
1976S Proof	4		.75			1.50
1977	797	...		...	.20	
1977D	377	...		...	.20	
1977S Proof	3		.75			1.50
1978	664	...		...	.20	
1978D	283	...		...	.20	
1978S Proof	3		.75			1.50
1979	315	...		...	.20	
1979D	391	...		...	.20	
1979S Proof	4					
Filled S			.60			1.00
Clear S			3.00			4.50
1980P	735	...		...	.20	
1980D	719	...		...	.20	
1980S Proof	4		.60			1.00
1981P	678	...		...	.20	
1981D	712	...		...	.20	
1981S Proof	4		.50			1.00
1982P		...		...	.20	
1982D		...		...	.20	
1982S Proof			.50			1.00

TWENTY CENT PIECES 1875-1878

This denomination was very unpopular because of its similarity to the 25c piece, and coinage for general circulation lasted only two years. Proof coins for collectors were made in 1877 and 1878. Most of the 1876CC issue was melted and only about ten specimens are in existence today. This is a very popular collectors' coin worth a premium in any condition. The edge is plain; weight 77.16 grains; .900 fine.

GOOD—*LIBERTY on shield obliterated. Letters and date legible.*
V. GOOD—*LIBERTY will not show. Other details will be bold.*
FINE—*At least 3 letters of LIBERTY show.*

Date	Thousands Minted	Avg. Dealers Pay Good	V. Good	Average Retail Prices Good	V. Good	Fine
1875	39	$32.50	$38.50	$50.00	$60.00	$75.00
1875CC	133	32.50	38.50	50.00	60.00	75.00
1875S	1,155	30.00	34.00	40.00	50.00	60.00
1876	16	40.00	60.00	70.00	90.00	120.00
1876CC	10	Rare				
1877		Rare				
1878		Rare				

QUARTER DOLLARS

The first quarters were issued in 1796. Design, weight, and fineness follow the pattern set by early half dimes and dimes. The edge is reeded. Mint marks, first used in 1840, are on the reverse below the eagle for all types through 1916. Arrows were added to the date in 1853-1855 and 1873-1874 to indicate the changes in weight.

Several minor varieties exist, some of them worth a premium. A number of overdates were issued.

QUARTERS
Draped Bust Type 1796-1807

FAIR—*Details clear enough to identify.*
GOOD—*Date readable. Bust outlined, but no detail.*
VERY GOOD—*All but deepest drapery folds worn smooth. Hairlines nearly gone and curls lack detail.*

Date	Thousands Minted	Avg. Dealers Pay		Average Retail Prices		
		Fair	Good	Fair	Good	V. Good
1796	6	$800.00	$1,500	$1,500	$2,750	$3,500

1804	7	150.00	200.00	300.00	600.00	700.00
1805	121	60.00	85.00	150.00	250.00	300.00
1806	206	50.00	75.00	150.00	250.00	300.00
1807	221	50.00	75.00	150.00	250.00	300.00

Capped Bust Type 1815-1828

FAIR—*Details clear enough to identify.*
GOOD—*Date, letters and stars readable. Hair under headband smooth. Cap lines worn smooth.*
VERY GOOD—*Rim well defined. Main details visible. Full LIBERTY on cap. Hair above eye nearly smooth.*

QUARTERS

Date	Thousands Minted	Avg. Dealers Pay		Average Retail Prices		
		Fair	Good	Fair	Good	V. Good
1815	89	$15.00	$22.00	$25.00	$45.00	$60.00
1818	361	13.00	20.00	25.00	45.00	60.00
1819	144	13.00	20.00	25.00	45.00	60.00
1820	127	13.00	20.00	25.00	45.00	60.00
1821	217	13.00	20.00	25.00	45.00	60.00
1822	64	13.00	20.00	25.00	45.00	60.00
1823	18	700.00	1,000	800.00	1,550	4,000
1824	} 168	16.00	23.00	30.00	50.00	65.00
1825		13.00	20.00	22.00	40.00	55.00
1827		Rare				
1828	102	13.00	20.00	22.00	40.00	50.00

Reduced size — No motto on reverse 1831-1838

GOOD—Bust is well defined. Hair under headband is smooth. Date, letters, stars readable. Scant rims.
VERY GOOD—Details apparent but worn on high spots. Rims strong. Full LIBERTY.
FINE—All hairlines visible. Drapery partly worn. Shoulder clasp distinct.

Date	Thousands Minted	Avg. Dealers Pay		Average Retail Prices		
		Good	V. Good	Good	V. Good	Fine
1831	398	20.00	27.00	36.00	45.00	55.00
1832	320	20.00	27.00	36.00	45.00	55.00
1833	156	22.00	30.00	40.00	50.00	70.00
1834	286	20.00	27.00	36.00	45.00	55.00
1835	1,952	20.00	27.00	36.00	45.00	55.00
1836	472	20.00	27.00	36.00	45.00	55.00
1837	252	20.00	27.00	36.00	45.00	55.00
1838	366	20.00	27.00	36.00	45.00	55.00

QUARTERS
Liberty Seated Type 1838-1891
Variety 1 — No motto above eagle 1838-1853

GOOD—Scant rim, LIBERTY on shield worn off. Date and letters readable.
V. GOOD—Rim fairly defined, at least 3 letters in LIBERTY evident.
FINE—Liberty complete, but partly weak.

Date	Thousands Minted	Avg. Dealers Pay Good	V. Good	Average Retail Prices Good	V. Good	Fine
1838	466	$5.50	$7.00	$11.00	$16.50	$25.00
1839	491	5.50	7.00	11.00	16.50	25.00
1840	188	5.00	6.00	12.00	15.00	20.00
1840O	425	5.00	6.00	12.00	15.00	20.00
1841	120	9.00	15.00	20.00	25.00	50.00
1841O	452	4.50	6.00	8.50	12.50	25.00
1842	88	12.00	25.00	60.00	80.00	125.00
1842O	769	4.50	6.00	14.00	18.00	25.00
1843	646	4.50	6.00	12.00	16.00	20.00
1843O	968	5.00	7.00	15.00	25.00	40.00
1844	421	4.50	6.00	12.00	16.00	25.00
1844O	740	4.50	6.00	12.00	16.00	25.00
1845	922	4.50	6.00	12.00	16.00	20.00
1846	510	4.50	6.00	12.00	16.00	25.00
1847	734	4.50	6.00	12.00	16.00	20.00
1847O	368	4.50	6.00	20.00	30.00	50.00
1848	146	7.00	15.00	16.00	25.00	50.00
1849	340	4.50	6.00	15.00	20.00	35.00
1849O		125.00	200.00	200.00	350.00	550.00
1850	191	4.50	6.00	12.00	20.00	30.00
1850O	412	4.50	6.00	25.00	35.00	50.00
1851	160	4.50	6.00	12.00	20.00	30.00
1851O	88	40.00	70.00	110.00	150.00	300.00
1852	177	4.50	6.00	20.00	30.00	50.00
1852O	96	90.00	165.00	200.00	300.00	400.00
1853	44	70.00	110.00	150.00	180.00	250.00

QUARTERS
Variety 2 — Arrows at date, rays around eagle 1853

Date	Thousands Minted	Avg. Dealers Pay Good	V. Good	Average Retail Prices Good	V. Good	Fine
1853	15,210	$6.00	$7.00	$10.00	$13.50	$18.00
1853O	1,332	6.50	8.00	11.00	15.00	25.00

Variety 3 — Arrows at date, no rays 1854-1855

1854	12,380	4.50	5.50	8.00	10.00	13.00
1854O	1,484	5.00	6.00	8.00	11.00	14.00
1855	2,857	5.00	6.00	8.00	11.00	14.00
1855O	176	25.00	35.00	45.00	65.00	95.00
1855S	396	25.00	35.00	45.00	65.00	95.00

Variety 1 resumed 1856-1865

1856	7,264	4.00	5.00	8.00	10.00	14.00
1856O	968	5.00	8.00	10.00	15.00	25.00
1856S	286	12.00	17.50	25.00	35.00	60.00
1857	9,644	4.00	5.00	8.00	10.00	14.00
1857O	1,180	4.00	5.50	9.00	11.50	16.00
1857S	82	15.00	30.00	30.00	60.00	125.00
1858	7,368	4.00	5.00	8.00	10.00	14.00
1858O	520	5.00	8.00	10.00	18.00	30.00
1858S	121	15.00	22.00	30.00	40.00	70.00
1859	1,344	4.00	5.00	8.00	10.00	14.00
1859O	260	6.00	9.00	12.00	20.00	35.00
1859S	80	18.00	27.50	40.00	60.00	120.00
1860	805	4.00	5.00	8.00	10.00	14.00
1860O	388	5.00	8.00	10.00	18.00	30.00
1860S	56	20.00	30.00	50.00	75.00	200.00
1861	4,855	4.00	5.00	8.00	10.00	14.00
1861S	96	13.50	18.00	25.00	35.00	60.00
1862	933	4.00	5.00	8.00	10.00	14.00
1862S	67	14.00	18.00	25.00	35.00	60.00
1863	192	6.00	9.00	16.00	20.00	30.00
1864	94	12.00	15.00	25.00	35.00	60.00
1864S	20	42.50	80.00	100.00	175.00	275.00
1865	59	15.00	21.00	32.00	45.00	80.00
1865S	41	15.00	20.00	30.00	40.00	70.00

QUARTERS
Variety 4 — Motto above eagle 1866-1873

Date	Thousands Minted	Avg. Dealers Pay Good	V. Good	Average Retail Prices Good	V. Good	Fine
1866	18	$40.00	$70.00	$100.00	$140.00	$200.00
1866S	28	16.00	22.50	40.00	50.00	125.00
1867	21	17.00	25.00	45.00	55.00	150.00
1867S	48	14.00	19.00	32.50	45.00	90.00
1868	30	12.00	20.00	35.00	50.00	100.00
1868S	96	12.00	17.00	25.00	35.00	65.00
1869	17	22.00	30.00	50.00	70.00	140.00
1869S	76	12.00	17.00	25.00	35.00	75.00
1870	87	10.00	15.00	25.00	32.50	50.00
1870CC	8	225.00	350.00	400.00	600.00	1,200
1871	119	4.50	5.50	10.00	14.00	25.00
1871CC	11	125.00	225.00	350.00	450.00	800.00
1871S	31	24.00	65.00	85.00	150.00	275.00
1872	183	4.00	5.00	8.50	12.50	20.00
1872CC	23	100.00	140.00	170.00	240.00	375.00
1872S	83	30.00	65.00	75.00	150.00	275.00
1873	213	4.00	7.00	10.00	20.00	35.00
1873CC	4	Rare				

Variety 5 — Arrows at date 1873-1874

1873	1,272	9.00	13.00	19.00	24.00	30.00
1873CC	12	200.00	275.00	400.00	500.00	750.00
1873S	156	11.00	15.00	20.00	25.00	40.00
1874	472	9.00	13.00	19.00	24.00	30.00
1874S	392	11.00	15.00	20.00	25.00	40.00

QUARTERS
Variety 4 resumed 1875-1891

Date	Thousands Minted	Avg. Dealers Pay Good	V. Good	Average Retail Prices Good	V. Good	Fine
1875	4,294	$4.00	$4.75	$8.00	$9.00	$11.00
1875CC	140	10.00	15.00	30.00	40.00	100.00
1875S	680	5.50	7.00	9.00	14.00	25.00
1876	17,817	4.00	4.75	8.00	9.00	11.00
1876CC	4,944	4.00	5.00	9.00	11.00	15.00
1876S	8,596	4.00	4.75	8.00	9.00	11.00
1877	10,912	4.00	4.75	8.00	9.00	11.00
1877CC	4,192	4.00	5.00	9.00	11.00	17.00
1877S	8,996	4.00	4.75	8.00	9.00	12.00
1878	2,261	4.00	4.75	8.00	9.00	12.00
1878CC	996	5.00	6.00	9.00	12.00	20.00
1878S	140	35.00	50.00	50.00	75.00	110.00
1879	15	25.00	33.00	65.00	75.00	110.00
1880	15	25.00	33.00	65.00	75.00	110.00
1881	13	25.00	33.00	65.00	75.00	110.00
1882	16	24.00	31.50	65.00	75.00	110.00
1883	15	24.00	31.50	65.00	75.00	110.00
1884	9	32.50	42.50	75.00	85.00	125.00
1885	15	24.00	31.50	65.00	75.00	110.00
1886	6	37.50	50.00	80.00	100.00	150.00
1887	11	35.00	44.00	65.00	75.00	110.00
1888	11	35.00	44.00	65.00	75.00	110.00
1888S	1,216	4.00	4.75	8.00	9.00	12.00
1889	13	25.00	33.00	65.00	75.00	110.00
1890	81	15.00	20.00	35.00	45.00	60.00
1891	3,921	4.00	4.75	8.00	9.00	12.00
1891O	68	50.00	65.00	110.00	125.00	200.00
1891S	2,216	4.50	5.25	8.00	10.00	15.00

Barber or Liberty Head Type 1892-1916

GOOD—*Date and legends readable. LIBERTY worn off headband.*
VERY GOOD—*Minimum of 3 letters in LIBERTY readable.*
FINE—*LIBERTY completely readable but not sharp.*

QUARTERS

Date	Thousands Minted	Avg. Dealers Pay		Average Retail Prices		
		Good	V. Good	Good	V. Good	Fine
1892	8,237	$2.00	$2.25	$3.00	$4.00	$9.00
1892O	2,640	3.00	4.50	4.00	9.00	18.00
1892S	964	7.00	12.00	13.00	19.00	30.00
1893	5,445	2.00	2.25	3.00	4.00	10.00
1893O	3,396	2.00	2.25	3.00	5.00	15.00
1893S	1,455	3.35	5.50	8.00	10.00	20.00
1894	3,433	2.00	2.25	3.00	5.00	10.00
1894O	2,852	2.00	2.25	3.00	5.00	15.00
1894S	2,649	2.00	2.25	3.00	5.00	15.00
1895	4,441	2.00	2.25	3.00	5.00	10.00
1895O	2,816	2.00	2.25	3.00	5.00	15.00
1895S	1,765	2.00	2.25	3.00	5.00	17.00
1896	3,875	2.00	2.25	3.00	5.00	10.00
1896O	1,484	4.00	5.00	7.50	8.00	20.00
1896S	188	175.00	200.00	275.00	325.00	650.00
1897	8,141	2.00	2.25	3.00	4.00	10.00
1897O	1,415	4.00	6.00	7.50	9.00	17.00
1897S	542	6.00	9.00	12.00	17.00	30.00
1898	11,101	2.00	2.25	3.00	4.00	9.00
1898O	1,868	2.00	2.25	3.00	4.00	12.00
1898S	1,021	2.00	2.25	3.00	4.00	10.00
1899	12,625	2.00	2.25	3.00	4.00	9.00
1899O	2,644	2.00	2.25	3.00	4.00	10.00
1899S	708	5.00	7.50	7.50	12.00	18.00
1900	10,017	2.00	2.25	3.00	4.00	9.00
1900O	3,416	2.00	6.00	4.00	9.00	16.00
1900S	1,859	2.00	2.25	3.00	4.00	9.00
1901	8,893	2.00	2.25	3.00	4.00	9.00
1901O	1,612	6.00	10.00	9.00	15.00	30.00
1901S	73	500.00	700.00	1,200	1,400	1,900
1902	12,198	2.00	2.25	3.00	4.00	9.00
1902O	4,748	2.00	2.25	3.00	4.00	9.00
1902S	1,525	2.00	6.50	4.00	10.00	17.00
1903	9,670	2.00	2.25	3.00	4.00	9.00
1903O	3,500	2.00	2.25	3.00	4.00	10.00
1903S	1,036	4.00	6.00	4.00	10.00	17.00
1904	9,589	2.00	2.25	3.00	4.00	9.00
1904O	2,456	2.00	5.00	4.00	8.00	15.00
1905	4,968	2.00	2.25	3.00	4.00	9.00
1905O	1,230	2.00	5.00	4.00	9.00	16.00
1905S	1,884	2.00	2.25	3.00	4.00	9.00
1906	3,656	2.00	2.25	3.00	4.00	9.00
1906D	3,280	2.00	2.25	3.00	4.00	9.00
1906O	2,056	2.00	2.25	3.00	4.00	9.00
1907	7,193	2.00	2.25	3.00	4.00	9.00
1907D	2,484	2.00	2.25	3.00	4.00	9.00
1907O	4,560	2.00	2.25	3.00	4.00	9.00
1907S	1,360	2.00	2.25	3.00	4.00	9.00

QUARTERS

Date	Thousands Minted	Avg. Dealers Pay		Average Retail Prices		
		Good	V. Good	Good	V. Good	Fine
1908	4,233	$2.00	$2.25	$3.00	$4.00	$9.00
1908D	5,788	2.00	2.25	3.00	4.00	9.00
1908O	6,244	2.00	2.25	3.00	4.00	9.00
1908S	784	2.00	6.00	3.70	10.00	17.00
1909	9,269	2.00	2.25	3.00	4.00	9.00
1909D	5,114	2.00	2.25	3.00	4.00	9.00
1909O	712	6.00	10.00	11.00	17.00	34.00
1909S	1,348	2.00	2.25	3.00	4.00	9.00
1910	2,245	2.00	2.25	3.00	4.00	9.00
1910D	1,500	2.00	2.25	3.00	4.00	10.00
1911	3,721	2.00	2.25	3.00	4.00	9.00
1911D	934	2.00	2.25	3.00	4.00	12.00
1911S	988	2.00	2.25	3.00	4.00	10.00
1912	4,441	2.00	2.25	3.00	4.00	9.00
1912S	708	2.00	2.25	3.00	4.00	10.00
1913	485	4.25	8.00	8.00	13.00	30.00
1913D	1,451	2.00	2.25	3.00	4.00	9.00
1913S	40	185.00	250.00	350.00	450.00	700.00
1914	6,245	2.00	2.25	3.00	4.00	9.00
1914D	3,046	2.00	2.25	3.00	4.00	9.00
1914S	264	6.00	10.00	12.00	16.00	27.50
1915	3,480	2.00	2.25	3.00	4.00	9.00
1915D	3,694	2.00	2.25	3.00	4.00	9.00
1915S	704	2.00	2.25	3.00	4.00	13.00
1916	1,788	2.00	2.25	3.00	4.00	9.00
1916D	6,541	2.00	2.25	3.00	4.00	9.00

Liberty Standing Type 1916-1930

The design of this coin, by Hermon MacNeil, was modified on two occasions: in 1917, when stars were placed below the eagle, and in 1925, when the pedestal with the date was recessed to prevent excessive wear. A variety of 1918S has the date engraved over 1917. These coins are generally found in worn condition and have no premium if the date does not show. Coins in new condition are worth considerably more than the prices shown. Mint marks are found on the obverse at left of date. The designer's initial M is at the right.

GOOD—Date and lettering readable. Top of date worn. Liberty's right leg and toes worn off. Left leg and drapery lines show much wear.
VERY GOOD—Distinct date. Toes show faintly. Drapery lines visible above her left leg.
FINE—High curve of right leg flat from thigh to ankle. Left leg shows only slight wear. Drapery lines over right thigh seen only at sides of leg.

QUARTERS

Variety 1 — No stars below eagle 1916-1917

Date	Thousands Minted	Avg. Dealers Pay Good	V. Good	Average Retail Prices Good	V. Good	Fine
1916	52	$400.00	$450.00	$1,300	$1,800	$2,400
1917	8,740	5.00	6.00	10.00	12.00	18.00
1917D	1,509	6.00	7.50	12.00	15.00	24.00
1917S	1,952	6.00	7.50	12.00	15.00	24.00

Variety 2 — Stars below eagle 1917-1930

1917	13,880	5.00	7.00	10.00	12.00	18.00
1917D	6,224	8.00	14.00	15.00	20.00	37.50
1917S	5,552	8.00	14.00	14.00	19.00	35.00
1918	14,240	5.50	8.00	12.00	16.00	25.00
1918D	7,380	8.00	15.00	18.00	25.00	40.00

1918S, 8 over 7

1918S	} 11,072	5.50	8.00	12.00	16.00	25.00
1918S, 8 over 7		600.00	750.00	1,200	1,750	2,500
1919	11,324	12.00	15.00	23.00	30.00	40.00
1919D	1,944	23.00	35.00	40.00	60.00	100.00
1919S	1,836	23.00	35.00	40.00	60.00	95.00
1920	27,860	5.00	7.00	10.00	13.00	19.00
1920D	3,586	10.00	15.00	20.00	25.00	45.00
1920S	6,380	5.50	7.50	12.00	15.00	24.00

QUARTERS

Date	Thousands Minted	Avg. Dealers Pay Good	V. Good	Average Retail Prices Good	V. Good	Fine
1921	1,916	$22.00	$32.00	$45.00	$65.00	$110.00
1923	9,716	5.00	7.00	10.00	15.00	19.00
1923S	1,360	32.00	55.00	70.00	95.00	145.00
1924	10,920	5.00	7.00	10.00	14.00	18.00
1924D	3,112	8.50	15.00	20.00	27.00	45.00
1924S	2,860	7.00	10.00	15.00	18.00	27.50
1925	12,280	2.00	2.25	3.00	3.70	9.00
1926	11,316	2.00	2.25	3.00	3.70	9.00
1926D	1,716	3.00	3.25	7.00	7.50	11.00
1926S	2,700	2.00	2.25	3.00	3.70	11.00
1927	11,912	2.00	2.25	3.00	3.70	9.00
1927D	976	3.00	3.25	7.50	10.00	15.00
1927S	396	6.50	12.00	15.00	25.00	100.00
1928	6,336	2.00	2.25	3.00	3.70	9.00
1928D	1,628	2.00	3.25	3.00	6.00	9.00
1928S	2,644	2.00	3.25	3.00	6.00	9.00
1929	11,140	2.00	2.25	3.00	4.00	9.00
1929D	1,358	2.00	2.25	3.00	6.00	10.00
1929S	1,764	2.00	3.25	3.00	6.00	10.00
1930	5,632	2.00	2.25	3.00	3.70	9.00
1930S	1,556	2.00	2.25	3.00	3.70	10.00

Washington Type 1932 to Date

Most Washington quarters are plentiful and worth a premium only for their silver content. Early dates are seldom found in sharp condition and values shown here are for grades most often encountered. The design, by John Flannagan, was used throughout the silver series and continued after 1965, when clad coinage started. Mint marks are below the wreath on the reverse of the silver coins and on the obverse of clad coins to the right of the ribbon. Clad coins from the San Francisco Mint were issued only in proof.

VERY GOOD—Wing-tips outlined. Rims on both sides are fine and even. Tops of letters at rim are flattened.
FINE—Hairlines around ear visible. Tiny feathers on eagle's breast faintly visible.
V. FINE—Hair details worn but plain. Feathers at sides of eagle's breast are plain.
EXTRA FINE—Hairlines sharp. Wear spots confined to top of eagle's legs and center of breast.

QUARTERS

Mint mark location
1932-1964

←

Date	Millions Minted	Avg. Dealers Pay		Average Retail Prices		
		V. Good	Fine	V. Good	Fine	V. Fine
1932	5	$1.50	$1.50	$2.00	$2.50	$3.40
1932D	0.4	38.00	50.00	45.00	55.00	80.00
1932S	0.4	36.00	45.00	42.50	50.00	70.00
1934	31	1.50	1.50	2.00	2.50	3.40
1934D	3	2.00	4.00	3.40	9.00	12.00
1935	32	1.50	1.50	2.00	2.50	3.40
1935D	5	1.50	1.50	2.00	2.50	3.40
1935S	5	1.50	1.50	2.00	2.50	3.40
1936	41	1.50	1.50	2.00	2.50	3.40
1936D	5	1.50	6.00	2.00	11.00	15.00
1936S	3	1.50	1.50	2.00	2.50	3.40
1937	19	1.50	1.50	2.00	2.50	3.40
1937D	7	1.50	1.50	2.00	2.50	3.40
1937S	1	3.50	5.00	8.00	10.00	12.00
1938	9	1.50	1.50	2.00	2.50	3.40
1938S	2	3.00	3.50	6.50	7.00	8.00
1939	33	1.50	1.50	2.00	2.50	3.40
1939D	7	1.50	1.50	2.00	2.50	3.40
1939S	2	3.00	3.50	3.50	6.50	7.00
1940	35	1.50	1.50	2.00	2.50	3.40
1940D	3	1.50	1.50	2.00	2.50	3.40
1940S	8	1.50	1.50	2.00	2.50	3.40
1941	79	1.50	1.50	2.00	2.50	3.40
1941D	17	1.50	1.50	2.00	2.50	3.40
1941S	16	1.50	1.50	2.00	2.50	3.40
1942	102	1.50	1.50	2.00	2.50	3.40
1942D	17	1.50	1.50	2.00	2.50	3.40
1942S	19	1.50	1.50	2.00	2.50	3.40
1943	100	1.50	1.50	2.00	2.50	3.40

> Common silver coins are worth a premium only for their silver content. This price may vary according to prevailing market value of silver bullion. See page 4 for details.

QUARTERS

Date	Millions Minted	Avg. Dealers Pay Fine	V. Fine	Average Retail Prices Fine	V. Fine	Ex. Fine
1943D	16	$1.50	$1.50	$2.00	$2.25	$7.50
1943S	22	1.50	1.50	2.00	2.25	7.50
1944	105	1.50	1.50	2.00	2.25	2.75
1944D	15	1.50	1.50	2.00	2.25	2.75
1944S	13	1.50	1.50	2.00	2.25	2.75
1945	74	1.50	1.50	2.00	2.25	2.75
1945D	12	1.50	1.50	2.00	2.25	2.75
1945S	17	1.50	1.50	2.00	2.25	2.75
1946	53	1.50	1.50	2.00	2.25	2.75
1946D	9	1.50	1.50	2.00	2.25	2.75
1946S	4	1.50	1.50	2.00	2.25	2.75
1947	23	1.50	1.50	2.00	2.25	2.75
1947D	15	1.50	1.50	2.00	2.25	2.75
1947S	6	1.50	1.50	2.00	2.25	2.75
1948	35	1.50	1.50	2.00	2.25	2.75
1948D	17	1.50	1.50	2.00	2.25	2.75
1948S	16	1.50	1.50	2.00	2.25	2.75
1949	9	1.50	1.50	2.00	2.25	2.75
1949D	10	1.50	1.50	2.00	2.25	2.75
1950	25	1.50	1.50	2.00	2.25	2.75
1950D	21	1.50	1.50	2.00	2.25	2.75
1950S	10	1.50	1.50	2.00	2.25	2.75
1951	44	1.50	1.50	2.00	2.25	2.50
1951D	35	1.50	1.50	2.00	2.25	2.50
1951S	9	1.50	1.50	2.00	2.25	2.50
1952	39	1.50	1.50	2.00	2.25	2.50
1952D	50	1.50	1.50	2.00	2.25	2.50
1952S	14	1.50	1.50	2.00	2.25	2.50
1953	19	1.50	1.50	2.00	2.25	2.50
1953D	56	1.50	1.50	2.00	2.25	2.50
1953S	14	1.50	1.50	2.00	2.25	2.50
1954	55	1.50	1.50	2.00	2.25	2.50
1954D	46	1.50	1.50	2.00	2.25	2.50
1954S	12	1.50	1.50	2.00	2.25	2.50
1955	19	1.50	1.50	2.00	2.25	2.50
1955D	3	1.50	1.50	2.00	2.25	2.50
1956	45	1.50	1.50	2.00	2.25	2.50
1956D	32	1.50	1.50	2.00	2.25	2.50
1957	48	1.50	1.50	2.00	2.25	2.50
1957D	78	1.50	1.50	2.00	2.25	2.50
1958	7	1.50	1.50	2.00	2.25	2.50
1958D	78	1.50	1.50	2.00	2.25	2.50
1959	26	1.50	1.50	2.00	2.25	2.50
1959D	62	1.50	1.50	2.00	2.25	2.50
1960	31	1.50	1.50	2.00	2.25	2.50
1960D	63	1.50	1.50	2.00	2.25	2.50
1961	40	1.50	1.50	2.00	2.25	2.50
1961D	84	1.50	1.50	2.00	2.25	2.50

QUARTERS

Date	Millions Minted	Avg. Dealers Pay Ex. Fine	Proof	Average Retail Prices Ex. Fine	Unc.	Proof
1962	39	*$1.50*	$3.00	*$2.50*	*$4.00*	$5.00
1962D	128	*1.50*		*2.50*	*4.00*	
1963	77	*1.50*	3.00	*2.50*	*4.00*	5.00
1963D	135	*1.50*		*2.50*	*4.00*	
1964	564	*1.50*	3.00	*2.50*	*4.00*	5.00
1964D	704	*1.50*		*2.50*	*4.00*	

CLAD COINAGE 1965-

Mint mark location starting 1968

1965	1,820	...		...	.50
1966	821	...		...	.50
1967	1,524	...		...	.50
1968	221	...		...	.50
1968D	102	...		...	1.00
1968S Proof	3		.50			1.00
1969	176	...		...	.50
1969D	114	...		...	1.25
1969S Proof	3		.50			1.00
1970	136	...		...	.50
1970D	417	...		...	.50
1970S Proof	3		.70			1.75
1971	109	...		...	.50
1971D	259	...		...	.50
1971S Proof	3		.50			1.00
1972	215	...		...	.50
1972D	311	...		...	.50
1972S Proof	3		.50			1.00
1973	347	...		...	.50
1973D	233	...		...	.50
1973S Proof	3		.70			1.75
1974	801	...		...	.50
1974D	353	...		...	.50
1974S Proof	3		.70			1.75

QUARTERS

BICENTENNIAL COINAGE DATED 1776-1976

The Bicentennial quarter was designed by Jack L. Ahr. It features a Colonial drummer facing left, with a victory torch encircled by thirteen stars at the upper left. Except for a dual dating, 1776-1976, the obverse remained unchanged.

Date	Millions Minted	Avg. Dealers Pay Ex. Fine	Proof	Average Retail Prices Ex. Fine	Unc.	Proof
1976	809	...		...	$ .50	
1976D	860	...		...	.50	
1976S Proof	7		$ .65			$1.75
1976S Silver	4	$1.20	1.75		1.75	4.00

Eagle Reverse Resumed

1977	467	...		...	.50	
1977D	257	...		...	.50	
1977S Proof	3		.50			1.00
1978	521	...		...	.50	
1978D	287	...		...	.50	
1978S Proof	3		.50			1.00
1979	516	...		...	.50	
1979D	490	...		...	.50	
1979S Proof	4					
Filled S			.50			1.00
Clear S			3.50			6.00
1980P	635	...		...	.50	
1980D	518	...		...	.50	
1980S Proof	4		.50			1.00
1981P	602	...		...	.50	
1981D	576	...		...	.50	
1981S Proof	4		.50			1.00
1982P		...		...	.50	
1982D		...		...	.50	
1982S Proof		...	.50	...		1.00

> Values shown in these listings are averages of prices quoted by dealers throughout the country. The publisher of this book does not buy, sell, or appraise coins.

HALF DOLLARS

The half dollar was authorized April 2, 1792 and was first coined in 1794, weight 208 grains, .892 fine. This was changed in 1837 to 206.25 grains, in 1853 to 192 grains, and in 1873 to 192.9. The alloy was changed in 1837 to .900 fine.

On the early coins, the edge is lettered FIFTY CENTS OR HALF A DOLLAR. From 1836 to the present, the edge is reeded. Minor varieties of the bust type half dollars are eagerly collected and some are worth an additional premium. There are numerous overdates in this series. The first branch mint halves were coined at New Orleans in 1838 and 1839. These have the mint mark above the date. All other halves, through 1915, have the mint mark on the reverse below the eagle. The weight changes of 1853 and 1873 are indicated by arrows at date.

Flowing Hair Type, Small Eagle 1794-1797

FAIR—*Clear enough to identify.*
GOOD—*Date and letters sufficient to be readable. Main devices outlined, but lack details.*
VERY GOOD—*Major details discernible. Letters well formed but worn.*

Date	Thousands Minted	Avg. Dealers Pay Fair	Good	Average Retail Prices Fair	Good	V. Good
1794	23	$200.00	$500.00	$450.00	$950.00	$1,400
1795	300	150.00	350.00	350.00	750.00	1,250

Bust Type, Small Eagle 1796-1797

1796 15 stars	4	3,000	5,000	7,500	10,000	13,000
16 stars	4	3,000	5,000	7,500	10,000	13,000
1797	4	3,000	5,000	7,500	10,000	13,000

HALF DOLLARS

Bust Type, Large Eagle 1801-1807

***GOOD**—Letters and date readable. E. PLURIBUS UNUM obliterated.*
***V. GOOD**—Motto partially readable. Only deepest drapery details visible. All other lines smooth.*
***FINE**—All drapery lines distinguishable. Hairlines near cheek and neck show some detail.*

Date	Thousands Minted	Avg. Dealers Pay		Average Retail Prices		
		Good	V. Good	Good	V. Good	Fine
1801	30	$65.00	$100.00	$150.00	$200.00	$400.00
1802	30	60.00	90.00	125.00	175.00	350.00
1803	188	40.00	50.00	115.00	160.00	250.00
1805	212	30.00	45.00	80.00	100.00	145.00
1806	840	25.00	40.00	75.00	90.00	135.00
1807	301	25.00	40.00	75.00	90.00	135.00

Capped Bust Type 1807-1839 Lettered Edge

***GOOD**—Date and letters readable. Bust worn smooth with outline distinct.*
***VERY GOOD**—LIBERTY visible but faint. Legends distinguishable. Clasp at shoulder visible. Curl above it nearly smooth.*
***FINE**—Clasp and adjacent curl clearly outlined with slight details.*

1807	751	16.00	18.00	35.00	45.00	60.00
1808	1,369	14.00	17.00	33.00	43.00	50.00
1809	1,406	14.00	16.00	27.00	38.00	45.00
1810	1,276	14.00	16.00	25.00	33.00	40.00

HALF DOLLARS

Date	Thousands Minted	Avg. Dealers Pay		Average Retail Prices		
		Good	V. Good	Good	V. Good	Fine
1811	1,204	$13.00	$15.00	$25.00	$31.00	$35.00
1812	1,628	13.00	15.00	25.00	31.00	35.00
1813	1,242	13.00	15.00	20.00	25.00	30.00
1814	1,039	13.00	15.00	20.00	25.00	30.00
1815	47	125.00	160.00	300.00	375.00	550.00
1817	1,216	13.00	15.00	20.00	23.00	27.50
1818	1,960	13.00	15.00	20.00	23.00	27.50
1819	2,208	13.00	15.00	21.00	24.00	30.00
1820	751	13.00	15.00	22.00	28.00	38.00
1821	1,306	13.00	15.00	20.00	22.00	30.00
1822	1,560	13.00	15.00	20.00	22.00	30.00
1823	1,694	13.00	15.00	19.00	21.00	26.00
1824	3,505	13.00	15.00	19.00	21.00	26.00
1825	2,943	13.00	15.00	19.00	21.00	26.00
1826	4,004	13.00	15.00	19.00	21.00	26.00
1827	5,493	13.00	15.00	19.00	21.00	26.00
1828	3,075	13.00	15.00	19.00	21.00	26.00
1829	3,712	13.00	15.00	19.00	21.00	26.00
1830	4,765	13.00	15.00	19.00	21.00	26.00
1831	5,874	13.00	15.00	19.00	21.00	26.00
1832	4,797	13.00	15.00	19.00	21.00	26.00
1833	5,206	13.00	15.00	19.00	21.00	26.00
1834	6,412	13.00	15.00	19.00	21.00	26.00
1835	5,352	13.00	15.00	19.00	21.00	26.00
1836	6,545	13.00	15.00	19.00	21.00	26.00

Reeded edge

GOOD—*LIBERTY discernible on headband.*
VERY GOOD—*Minimum of 3 letters in LIBERTY must be clear.*
FINE—*LIBERTY complete.*

1836	1	150.00	200.00	300.00	400.00	500.00
1837	3,630	17.50	22.50	30.00	40.00	55.00
1838	3,546	15.00	20.00	30.00	40.00	55.00
1838O		Rare				
1839	3,335	15.00	20.00	30.00	40.00	55.00
1839O	179	45.00	80.00	100.00	150.00	200.00

HALF DOLLARS
Liberty Seated Type

***GOOD**—Scant rim, LIBERTY on shield worn off. Date and letters readable.*
***VERY GOOD**—Rim fairly defined. At least 3 letters in LIBERTY are evident.*
***FINE**—LIBERTY complete, but weak.*

Date	Thousands Minted	Avg. Dealers Pay Good	V. Good	Average Retail Prices Good	V. Good	Fine
1839	.....	$8.50	$10.00	$22.50	$27.50	$35.00
1840	1,435	7.50	9.00	20.00	25.00	30.00
1840O	855	7.50	9.00	20.00	25.00	30.00
1841	310	9.50	11.00	22.00	26.00	30.00
1841O	401	7.50	9.00	20.00	25.00	30.00
1842	2,013	7.50	9.00	20.00	25.00	30.00
1842O	957	7.50	9.00	20.00	23.00	25.00
1843	3,844	7.50	9.00	20.00	23.00	25.00
1843O	2,268	7.50	9.00	20.00	23.00	25.00
1844	1,766	7.50	9.00	20.00	23.00	25.00
1844O	2,005	7.50	9.00	20.00	23.00	25.00
1845	589	7.50	9.00	20.00	23.00	25.00
1845O	2,094	7.50	9.00	20.00	23.00	25.00
1846	2,210	7.50	9.00	20.00	23.00	25.00
1846O	2,304	7.50	9.00	20.00	23.00	25.00
1847	1,156	7.50	9.00	20.00	23.00	25.00
1847O	2,584	7.50	9.00	20.00	23.00	25.00
1848	580	10.00	14.00	30.00	40.00	60.00
1848O	3,180	7.50	9.00	20.00	23.00	25.00
1849	1,252	7.50	9.00	20.00	23.00	25.00
1849O	2,310	7.50	9.00	20.00	23.00	25.00
1850	227	15.00	21.00	35.00	50.00	70.00
1850O	2,456	7.50	9.00	20.00	23.00	25.00
1851	201	15.00	21.00	35.00	50.00	70.00
1851O	402	7.50	9.00	20.00	23.00	25.00
1852	77	22.50	35.00	65.00	80.00	125.00
1852O	144	15.00	21.00	35.00	50.00	70.00
1853O	.....	Rare				

HALF DOLLARS
Arrows added to date

Date	Thousands Minted	Avg. Dealers Pay		Average Retail Prices		
		Good	V. Good	Good	V. Good	Fine
1853	3,533	$9.00	$12.50	$22.50	$27.50	$35.00
1853O	1,328	9.00	12.50	22.50	27.50	35.00
1854	2,982	8.00	10.00	20.00	22.50	25.00
1854O	5,240	8.00	10.00	20.00	22.50	25.00
1855	760	8.00	10.00	20.00	22.50	26.00
1855O	3,688	8.00	10.00	20.00	22.50	25.00
1855S	130	35.00	70.00	110.00	135.00	225.00

Arrows not used after 1855

Date	Thousands Minted	Good	V. Good	Good	V. Good	Fine
1856	938	7.50	9.00	19.00	21.00	24.00
1856O	2,658	7.50	9.00	19.00	21.00	24.00
1856S	211	9.50	11.00	22.00	25.00	35.00
1857	1,988	7.50	9.00	19.00	21.00	24.00
1857O	818	7.50	9.00	19.00	21.00	24.00
1857S	158	9.00	13.00	25.00	33.00	45.00
1858	4,226	7.50	9.00	19.00	21.00	24.00
1858O	7,294	7.50	9.00	19.00	21.00	24.00
1858S	476	8.50	10.00	21.00	25.00	30.00
1859	748	7.50	9.00	19.00	21.00	24.00
1859O	2,834	7.50	9.00	19.00	21.00	24.00
1859S	566	7.50	9.00	21.00	25.00	30.00
1860	304	7.50	9.00	21.00	25.00	27.50
1860O	1,290	7.50	9.00	19.00	21.00	24.00
1860S	472	8.50	11.00	21.00	24.00	27.00
1861	2,888	7.50	9.00	19.00	21.00	24.00
1861O	2,533	7.50	9.00	19.00	21.00	24.00
1861S	940	7.50	9.00	19.00	21.00	24.00
1862	254	9.50	13.00	22.50	30.00	35.00
1862S	1,352	7.50	9.00	19.00	21.00	24.00
1863	504	7.50	9.00	21.00	24.00	27.00
1863S	916	7.50	9.00	19.00	21.00	24.00
1864	380	7.50	9.00	21.00	24.00	27.00
1864S	658	7.50	9.00	19.00	21.00	24.00
1865	512	7.50	9.00	21.00	24.00	27.00
1865S	675	7.50	9.00	19.00	21.00	24.00
1866S	1,054	22.50	37.50	45.00	75.00	135.00

HALF DOLLARS

Date	Thousands Minted	Avg. Dealers Pay Good	V. Good	Average Retail Prices Good	V. Good	Fine
1866	746	$7.00	$8.00	$13.00	$15.00	$20.00
1866S		7.00	8.00	13.00	15.00	20.00
1867	450	7.00	8.00	15.00	17.00	20.00
1867S	1,196	7.00	8.00	13.00	15.00	20.00
1868	418	7.00	8.00	13.00	15.00	20.00
1868S	1,160	7.00	8.00	13.00	15.00	20.00
1869	796	7.00	8.00	13.00	15.00	20.00
1869S	656	7.00	8.00	13.00	15.00	20.00
1870	635	7.00	8.00	13.00	15.00	20.00
1870CC	55	75.00	125.00	170.00	300.00	600.00
1870S	1,004	7.00	8.00	13.00	15.00	20.00
1871	1,205	7.00	8.00	13.00	15.00	20.00
1871CC	154	24.00	35.00	50.00	75.00	135.00
1871S	2,178	7.00	8.00	13.00	15.00	20.00
1872	882	7.00	8.00	19.00	21.00	24.00
1872CC	257	15.00	22.50	32.50	55.00	85.00
1872S	580	7.00	8.00	13.00	15.00	20.00
1873	802	7.00	8.00	13.00	15.00	20.00
1873CC	123	21.00	35.00	50.00	75.00	135.00

Arrows added to date

Date	Thousands Minted	Good	V. Good	Good	V. Good	Fine
1873	1,816	10.00	16.00	23.00	30.00	45.00
1873CC	215	16.00	25.00	32.50	55.00	100.00
1873S	228	14.50	24.00	30.00	35.00	60.00
1874	2,360	10.00	16.00	23.00	30.00	45.00
1874CC	59	21.00	37.50	45.00	75.00	200.00
1874S	394	16.00	24.00	30.00	45.00	75.00

Arrows removed after 1874

Date	Thousands Minted	Good	V. Good	Good	V. Good	Fine
1875	6,028	7.00	8.00	13.00	15.00	20.00
1875CC	1,008	7.50	9.50	14.00	17.00	25.00
1875S	3,200	7.00	8.00	13.00	15.00	20.00
1876	8,419	7.00	8.00	13.00	15.00	20.00
1876CC	1,956	7.00	8.00	14.00	16.00	22.00
1876S	4,528	7.00	8.00	13.00	15.00	20.00
1877	8,305	7.00	8.00	13.00	15.00	20.00
1877CC	1,420	8.00	9.00	14.00	16.00	22.00
1877S	5,356	7.00	8.00	13.00	15.00	20.00
1878	1,378	7.00	8.00	13.00	15.00	20.00
1878CC	62	55.00	75.00	150.00	225.00	350.00
1878S	12	800.00	1,100	2,000	2,750	3,500
1879	6	50.00	60.00	100.00	110.00	200.00
1880	10	45.00	55.00	90.00	100.00	180.00
1881	11	42.50	52.50	90.00	100.00	180.00
1882	6	50.00	60.00	100.00	110.00	200.00
1883	9	45.00	55.00	90.00	100.00	180.00
1884	5	50.00	60.00	100.00	110.00	200.00
1885	6	50.00	60.00	90.00	100.00	180.00
1886	6	55.00	65.00	90.00	100.00	180.00

HALF DOLLARS

Date	Thousands Minted	Avg. Dealers Pay Good	V. Good	Average Retail Prices Good	V. Good	Fine
1887	6	$50.00	$60.00	$90.00	$100.00	$180.00
1888	13	35.00	45.00	85.00	90.00	150.00
1889	13	35.00	45.00	85.00	90.00	150.00
1890	13	35.00	45.00	85.00	90.00	150.00
1891	201	7.00	8.00	13.00	15.00	22.50

Barber or Liberty Head Type 1892-1915

GOOD—Date and legends readable. LIBERTY worn off headband.
VERY GOOD—Minimum of 3 letters readable in LIBERTY.
FINE—LIBERTY completely readable, but not sharp.

Date	Millions Minted	Avg. Dealers Pay Good	V. Good	Average Retail Prices Good	V. Good	Fine
1892	0.9	6.50	11.00	14.00	21.00	40.00
1892O	0.4	65.00	75.00	100.00	125.00	150.00
1892S	1	60.00	70.00	100.00	120.00	130.00
1893	2	5.00	8.00	13.00	16.00	26.00
1893O	1	9.00	13.00	17.00	25.00	45.00
1893S	0.7	31.00	35.00	50.00	75.00	125.00
1894	1	5.00	8.00	13.00	17.00	30.00
1894O	2	5.00	8.00	13.00	17.00	30.00
1894S	4	5.00	6.50	8.00	12.00	25.00
1895	2	5.00	6.50	8.00	12.00	23.00
1895O	2	6.50	8.00	13.00	19.00	35.00
1895S	1	9.50	12.00	17.00	25.00	45.00
1896	1	5.00	6.50	8.00	12.00	30.00
1896O	0.9	7.50	13.00	17.00	25.00	45.00
1896S	1	30.00	38.00	50.00	70.00	90.00
1897	2	5.00	6.50	8.00	10.00	21.00
1897O	0.6	25.00	30.00	50.00	65.00	90.00
1897S	0.9	27.00	40.00	70.00	90.00	140.00
1898	3	5.00	6.50	8.00	10.00	21.00
1898O	0.9	7.50	12.00	15.00	25.00	45.00
1898S	2	5.00	6.50	10.00	14.00	30.00
1899	6	5.00	6.50	8.00	10.00	21.00
1899O	2	5.00	6.50	8.00	10.00	22.00

HALF DOLLARS

Date	Millions Minted	Avg. Dealers Pay Good	V. Good	Average Retail Prices Good	V. Good	Fine
1899S	2	$6.50	$8.00	$13.00	$18.00	$32.00
1900	5	4.00	5.00	7.00	8.00	20.00
1900O	3	4.00	5.00	7.00	8.00	25.00
1900S	3	4.00	5.00	7.00	8.00	24.00
1901	4	4.00	5.00	7.00	8.00	20.00
1901O	1	4.00	5.00	7.00	9.00	30.00
1901S	0.8	10.00	13.00	17.00	22.00	40.00
1902	5	4.00	5.00	7.00	8.00	20.00
1902O	3	4.00	5.00	7.00	8.00	20.00
1902S	1	4.00	5.00	7.00	8.00	20.00
1903	2	4.00	5.00	7.00	8.00	20.00
1903O	2	4.00	5.00	7.00	8.00	20.00
1903S	2	4.00	5.00	7.00	8.00	20.00
1904	3	4.00	5.00	7.00	8.00	20.00
1904O	1	4.00	5.00	7.00	9.00	32.00
1904S	0.6	10.00	13.00	15.00	22.00	45.00
1905	0.7	4.00	5.00	7.00	10.00	35.00
1905O	0.5	4.00	6.50	8.00	17.50	40.00
1905S	2	4.00	5.00	7.00	8.00	20.00
1906	3	4.00	5.00	7.00	8.00	20.00
1906D	4	4.00	5.00	7.00	8.00	20.00
1906O	2	4.00	5.00	7.00	8.00	20.00
1906S	2	4.00	5.00	7.00	8.00	20.00
1907	3	4.00	5.00	7.00	8.00	20.00
1907D	4	4.00	5.00	7.00	8.00	20.00
1907O	4	4.00	5.00	7.00	8.00	20.00
1907S	1	4.00	5.00	7.00	8.00	20.00
1908	1	4.00	5.00	7.00	8.00	20.00
1908D	3	4.00	5.00	7.00	8.00	20.00
1908O	5	4.00	5.00	7.00	8.00	20.00
1908S	2	4.00	5.00	7.00	8.00	20.00
1909	2	4.00	5.00	7.00	8.00	20.00
1909O	0.9	4.00	5.00	7.00	8.00	25.00
1909S	2	4.00	5.00	7.00	8.00	20.00
1910	0.4	4.00	11.00	10.00	19.00	35.00
1910S	2	4.00	5.00	7.00	8.00	20.00
1911	1	4.00	5.00	7.00	8.00	20.00
1911D	0.7	4.00	5.00	7.00	8.00	20.00
1911S	1	4.00	5.00	7.00	8.00	20.00
1912	2	4.00	5.00	7.00	8.00	20.00
1912D	2	4.00	5.00	7.00	8.00	20.00
1912S	1	4.00	5.00	7.00	8.00	20.00
1913	0.2	10.00	17.00	20.00	30.00	60.00
1913D	0.5	4.00	5.00	7.00	8.00	20.00
1913S	0.6	4.00	5.00	7.00	8.00	20.00
1914	0.1	14.00	17.00	25.00	37.00	70.00
1914S	1	4.00	5.00	7.00	8.00	20.00
1915	0.1	11.00	15.00	22.50	32.50	65.00
1915D	1	4.00	5.00	7.00	8.00	20.00
1915S	2	4.00	5.00	7.00	8.00	20.00

HALF DOLLARS
Liberty Walking Type 1916-1947

Many of the dates in this series are still commonly available and worth only their silver value. Early dates are seldom found in high grade condition. Those minted in 1916 and early 1917 have the mint mark on the obverse. Late in 1917 and for the rest of the series the mint mark is on the reverse at the lower left side. The design is by A. A. Weinman, whose monogram is on the reverse side.

GOOD—Rims are defined. Motto IN GOD WE TRUST readable.
VERY GOOD—Motto is distinct. About half of skirt lines at left are clear.
FINE—All skirt lines evident, but worn in spots. Details in sandal below motto are clear.
VERY FINE—Skirt lines sharp including leg area. Little wear on breast and arm.

Date	Millions Minted	Avg. Dealers Pay Good	V. Good	Average Retail Prices Good	V. Good	Fine
1916	0.6	$8.00	$11.00	$18.00	$25.00	$50.00
1916D on obv	1	6.50	8.50	15.00	20.00	25.00
1916S on obv	0.5	14.00	19.00	27.00	40.00	90.00
1917	12	3.00	3.25	5.00	6.00	8.00
1917D on obv	0.8	6.50	8.50	14.00	20.00	30.00
1917D on rev	2	3.00	3.25	9.00	12.00	25.00
1917S on obv	1	7.00	8.50	15.00	20.00	40.00
1917S on rev	6	3.00	3.25	5.00	7.00	8.00
1918	7	3.00	3.25	5.00	7.00	8.00
1918D	4	3.00	3.25	5.00	7.00	8.00
1918S	10	3.00	3.25	5.00	7.00	8.00
1919	1	3.00	3.25	10.00	15.00	31.00
1919D	1	3.00	3.25	10.00	15.00	31.00
1919S	2	3.00	3.25	7.00	9.00	20.00
1920	6	3.00	3.25	5.00	7.00	8.00
1920D	2	3.00	3.25	8.00	10.00	25.00
1920S	5	3.00	3.25	7.00	9.00	20.00
1921	0.2	24.00	32.00	55.00	90.00	160.00
1921D	0.2	40.00	50.00	85.00	125.00	270.00
1921S	0.5	8.00	13.50	17.50	30.00	45.00
1923S	2	3.00	3.00	5.00	7.00	8.00
1927S	2	3.00	3.00	5.00	7.00	8.00

HALF DOLLARS

Date	Millions Minted	Avg. Dealers Pay Good	V. Good	Average Retail Prices Good	V. Good	Fine
1928S	2	$3.00	$3.00	$5.00	$6.00	$7.00
1929D	1	3.00	3.00	5.00	6.00	7.00
1929S	2	3.00	3.00	5.00	6.00	7.00
1933S	2	3.00	3.00	5.00	6.00	7.00
1934	7	3.00	3.00	5.00	6.00	7.00
1934D	2	3.00	3.00	5.00	6.00	7.00
1934S	4	3.00	3.00	5.00	6.00	7.00
1935	9	3.00	3.00	5.00	6.00	7.00
1935D	3	3.00	3.00	5.00	6.00	7.00
1935S	4	3.00	3.00	5.00	6.00	7.00
1936	13	3.00	3.00	5.00	6.00	7.00
1936D	4	3.00	3.00	5.00	6.00	7.00
1936S	4	3.00	3.00	5.00	6.00	7.00
1937	10	3.00	3.00	5.00	6.00	7.00
1937D	2	3.00	3.00	5.00	6.00	7.00
1937S	2	3.00	3.00	5.00	6.00	7.00
1938	4	3.00	3.00	5.00	6.00	7.00
1938D	0.5	14.00	15.00	24.00	27.00	30.00
1939	7	3.00	3.00	5.00	6.00	7.00
1939D	4	3.00	3.00	5.00	6.00	7.00
1939S	3	3.00	3.00	5.00	6.00	7.00
1940	9	3.00	3.00	5.00	6.00	7.00
1940S	5	3.00	3.00	5.00	6.00	7.00

Date	Millions Minted	Avg. Dealers Pay V. Good	Fine	Average Retail Prices V. Good	Fine	V. Fine
1941	24	3.00	3.00	5.00	6.00	7.00
1941D	11	3.00	3.00	5.00	6.00	7.00
1941S	8	3.00	3.00	5.00	6.00	7.00
1942	48	3.00	3.00	5.00	6.00	7.00
1942D	11	3.00	3.00	5.00	6.00	7.00
1942S	13	3.00	3.00	5.00	6.00	7.00
1943	53	3.00	3.00	5.00	6.00	7.00
1943D	11	3.00	3.00	5.00	6.00	7.00
1943S	13	3.00	3.00	5.00	6.00	7.00
1944	28	3.00	3.00	5.00	6.00	7.00
1944D	10	3.00	3.00	5.00	6.00	7.00
1944S	9	3.00	3.00	5.00	6.00	7.00
1945	32	3.00	3.00	5.00	6.00	7.00
1945D	10	3.00	3.00	5.00	6.00	7.00
1945S	10	3.00	3.00	5.00	6.00	7.00
1946	12	3.00	3.00	5.00	6.00	7.00
1946D	2	3.00	3.00	5.00	6.00	7.00
1946S	4	3.00	3.00	5.00	6.00	7.00
1947	4	3.00	3.00	5.00	6.00	7.00
1947D	4	3.00	3.00	5.00	6.00	7.00

Common silver coins are worth a premium only for their silver content. This price may vary according to prevailing market value of silver bullion. See page 4 for details.

HALF DOLLARS
Franklin Type 1948-1963

FINE—Designer's initials distinct and clear.
V. FINE—Half of incused lines on bell show.
EX. FINE—Wear spots appear at top of end curls and hair back of ears. On reverse, Liberty bell will show wear at top.

Date	Millions Minted	Avg. Dealers Pay Fine	V. Fine	Average Retail Prices Fine	V. Fine	Ex. Fine
1948	3	$3.00	$3.00	$4.00	$4.50	$7.00
1948D	4	3.00	3.00	4.00	4.50	7.00
1949	6	3.00	3.50	7.00	8.00	10.00
1949D	4	3.00	3.50	4.00	7.00	10.00
1949S	4	3.00	3.50	4.00	7.00	17.50
1950	8	3.00	3.00	4.00	4.50	7.00
1950D	8	3.00	3.00	4.00	4.50	7.00
1951	17	3.00	3.00	4.00	4.50	7.00
1951D	9	3.00	3.00	4.00	4.50	4.75
1951S	14	3.00	3.00	4.00	4.50	4.75
1952	21	3.00	3.00	4.00	4.50	4.75
1952D	25	3.00	3.00	4.00	4.50	4.75
1952S	6	3.00	3.00	4.00	4.50	4.75
1953	3	3.00	3.00	4.00	4.50	4.75
1953D	21	3.00	3.00	4.00	4.50	4.75
1953S	4	3.00	3.00	4.00	4.50	4.75
1954	13	3.00	3.00	4.00	4.50	4.75
1954D	25	3.00	3.00	4.00	4.50	4.75
1954S	5	3.00	3.00	4.00	4.50	4.75
1955	3	3.00	3.00	4.00	4.50	4.75
1956	5	3.00	3.00	4.00	4.50	4.75
1957	6	3.00	3.00	4.00	4.50	4.75
1957D	20	3.00	3.00	4.00	4.50	4.75
1958	5	3.00	3.00	4.00	4.50	4.75
1958D	24	3.00	3.00	4.00	4.50	4.75
1959	7	3.00	3.00	4.00	4.50	4.75
1959D	13	3.00	3.00	4.00	4.50	4.75
1960	8	3.00	3.00	4.00	4.50	4.75
1960D	18	3.00	3.00	4.00	4.50	4.75
1961	11	3.00	3.00	4.00	4.50	4.75
1961D	20	3.00	3.00	4.00	4.50	4.75
1962	13	3.00	3.00	4.00	4.50	4.75
1962D	35	3.00	3.00	4.00	4.50	4.75
1963	25	3.00	3.00	4.00	4.50	4.75
1963D	67	3.00	3.00	4.00	4.50	4.75

HALF DOLLARS

Kennedy Type 1964 to Date

Despite a large coinage, many half dollars of this type have been saved as souvenirs which has limited their circulation. Those dated 1964 are made of 90% silver. This was changed in 1965 to a clad composition that has an outer layer of 80% silver bonded to an inner core of 21% silver, for a total of 40% silver. In 1971 the composition was again changed, this time to a copper core with outer layers of copper-nickel.

The mint mark is left of the olive branch on the reverse in 1964 and on the obverse above the date thereafter. San Francisco coins were made only as proofs and not for circulation.

***EX. FINE**—Small amount of wear on hair above ear. Wear spots also on jawbone, cheek and top of ear.*

Date	Millions Minted	Avg. Dealers Pay Ex. Fine	Proof	Ex. Fine	Average Retail Prices Unc.	Proof
1964	277	$3.00	$7.00	$4.50	$5.00	$10.00
1964D	156	3.00		4.50	5.00	

SILVER CLAD COINAGE 1965-1970

1965	66	.90		1.25	3.00	
1966	109	.90		1.25	3.00	
1967	295	.90		1.25	3.00	
1968D	247	.90		1.25	3.00	
1968S Proof	3		3.00			5.00
1969D	130	.90		1.25	3.00	
1969S Proof	3		3.00			5.00
1970D	2	12.00		30.00	40.00	
1970S Proof	3		6.00			10.00

COPPER-NICKEL CLAD COINAGE 1971-1974, 1977-

1971	155	...		...	1.00	
1971D	302	...		...	1.00	
1971S Proof	3		2.00			4.00
1972	153	...		...	1.00	
1972D	142	...		...	1.00	
1972S Proof	3		2.00			4.00
1973	65	...		...	1.00	
1973D	83	...		...	1.00	

HALF DOLLARS

Date	Millions Minted	Avg. Dealers Pay Ex. Fine	Proof	Average Retail Prices Ex. Fine	Unc.	Proof
1973S Proof	3		$3.00			$5.00
1974	201	...		...	$1.00	
1974D	79	...		...	1.00	
1974S Proof	3		3.00			5.00
1977	43	...		...	.75	
1977D	31	...		...	.75	
1977S Proof	3		2.50			4.00
1978	14	...		...	2.00	
1978D	14	...		...	1.75	
1978S Proof	3		2.50			4.50
1979	68	...		...	.75	
1979D	16	...		...	.75	
1979S Proof	4					
Filled S			2.00			3.00
Clear S			45.00			65.00
1980P	44	...		...	.75	
1980D	33	...		...	.75	
1980S Proof	4		2.00			3.00
1981P	30	...		...	.75	
1981D	28	...		...	.75	
1981S Proof	4		2.00			3.00
1982P		...		...	.75	
1982D		...		...	.75	
1982S Proof			11.00			16.00

BICENTENNIAL COINAGE DATED 1776-1976

In October 1973 the Treasury announced an open contest for the selection of suitable designs for the special Bicentennial reverses of the quarter, half dollar and dollar. Seth G. Huntington's winning entry is featured on the half dollar. It shows Independence Hall in Philadelphia as the center device. The obverse is unchanged except for the dual dating 1776-1976.

The mint mark is on the obverse above the date. San Francisco coins were made only for the sets and not for circulation.

1976	234	...		...	1.00	
1976D	287	...		...	1.00	
1976S	7		2.00			4.00
1976S Silver	4	3.00	3.50		6.00	7.00

SILVER DOLLARS

The silver dollar was authorized by Congress April 2, 1792. Weight and fineness were specified at 416 grains and 892.4 thousandths. The first date, 1794, is quite rare. There have been only a few changes in design over the years, but there are many minor varieties of the early dates. From 1794 to 1804 the edge is lettered HUNDRED CENTS ONE DOLLAR OR UNIT. All others have a reeded edge. The 1804 dollar is one of the rarest and most discussed coins in American numismatics. Pattern or trial pieces dated 1836-1838 are known to exist. The weight was changed by law in 1837 to 412.5 grains, .900 fine.

Liberty Seated dollars are rarely found. Mint marks on these appear on the reverse below the eagle.

Flowing Hair Type 1794-1795

FAIR—Clear enough to identify.
GOOD—Date and letters readable. Main devices outlined, but lack details.
V. GOOD—Major details discernible. Letters well formed but worn.

Date	Thousands Minted	Avg. Dealers Pay Fair	Good	Average Retail Prices Fair	Good	V. Good
1794	2	$1,500	$3,000	$3,000	$5,000	$7,500
1795	160	325.00	750.00	800.00	1,750	2,500

[98]

SILVER DOLLARS
Draped Bust Type 1795-1798
Small eagle reverse

FAIR—Clear enough to identify.
GOOD—Bust outlined, no detail. Date readable, some leaves evident.
V. GOOD—Drapery worn except deepest folds. Hairlines smooth.

Date	Thousands Minted	Avg. Dealers Pay Good	V. Good	Average Retail Prices Good	V. Good	Fine
1795	43	$500.00	$800.00	$1,400	$2,000	$2,750
1796	73	400.00	650.00	1,000	1,500	2,000
1797	8	400.00	650.00	1,000	1,500	2,000
1798	328	400.00	675.00	1,200	1,750	2,400

Heraldic eagle reverse 1798-1804

1798		200.00	275.00	375.00	450.00	600.00
1799	424	200.00	275.00	375.00	450.00	600.00
1800	221	200.00	275.00	375.00	450.00	600.00
1801	54	200.00	275.00	375.00	450.00	600.00
1802	42	200.00	275.00	375.00	450.00	600.00
1803	86	200.00	275.00	375.00	450.00	600.00
1804		Rare				

SILVER DOLLARS
Liberty Seated Type 1840-1873

V. GOOD—*Any three letters of LIBERTY should be at least two-thirds complete.*
FINE—*All drapery lines show but partly worn. Hair from brow, over ear and down neck, well outlined but shows only slight detail.*
V. FINE—*LIBERTY is strong and its ribbon shows slight wear.*

Date	Thousands Minted	Avg. Dealers Pay V. Good	Fine	Average Retail Prices V. Good	Fine	V. Fine
1840	61	$80.00	$100.00	$120.00	$150.00	$225.00
1841	173	70.00	90.00	110.00	135.00	200.00
1842	185	70.00	90.00	110.00	135.00	200.00
1843	165	70.00	90.00	110.00	135.00	200.00
1844	20	100.00	125.00	175.00	200.00	275.00
1845	25	90.00	110.00	150.00	175.00	250.00
1846	111	70.00	90.00	110.00	135.00	200.00
1846O	59	100.00	125.00	185.00	210.00	285.00
1847	141	70.00	90.00	110.00	135.00	200.00
1848	15	120.00	170.00	200.00	300.00	400.00
1849	63	85.00	110.00	130.00	170.00	250.00
1850	8	150.00	200.00	250.00	350.00	500.00
1850O	40	120.00	170.00	200.00	300.00	400.00
1851	1	Rare				
1852	1	Rare				
1853	46	85.00	110.00	130.00	170.00	250.00
1854	33	150.00	200.00	250.00	350.00	500.00
1855	26	150.00	200.00	250.00	350.00	500.00
1856	64	90.00	110.00	150.00	175.00	250.00
1857	94	90.00	110.00	150.00	175.00	250.00
1858		Rare				
1859	257	60.00	80.00	95.00	120.00	170.00
1859O	360	60.00	80.00	85.00	110.00	150.00
1859S	20	85.00	110.00	135.00	175.00	250.00

SILVER DOLLARS

Date	Thousands Minted	Avg. Dealers Pay V. Good	Fine	Average Retail Prices V. Good	Fine	V. Fine
1860	219	$70.00	$90.00	$110.00	$135.00	$200.00
1860O	515	60.00	80.00	85.00	110.00	150.00
1861	79	85.00	110.00	130.00	170.00	250.00
1862	12	120.00	175.00	225.00	325.00	450.00
1863	28	80.00	100.00	125.00	150.00	200.00
1864	31	80.00	100.00	125.00	150.00	200.00
1865	47	80.00	100.00	125.00	150.00	200.00

1866	50	70.00	100.00	100.00	150.00	200.00
1867	48	70.00	100.00	100.00	150.00	200.00
1868	163	60.00	85.00	85.00	130.00	170.00
1869	424	60.00	85.00	85.00	130.00	170.00
1870	416	60.00	85.00	85.00	130.00	170.00
1870CC	12	100.00	200.00	175.00	250.00	400.00
1870S		Rare				
1871	1,075	60.00	80.00	75.00	125.00	150.00
1871CC	1	375.00	700.00	700.00	1,200	2,000
1872	1,106	60.00	80.00	75.00	125.00	150.00
1872CC	3	200.00	350.00	350.00	500.00	900.00
1872S	9	100.00	200.00	175.00	275.00	450.00
1873	294	60.00	80.00	75.00	125.00	150.00
1873CC	2	500.00	700.00	750.00	1,000	1,500

> Values shown in these listings are averages of prices quoted by dealers throughout the country. The publisher of this book does not buy, sell, or appraise coins.

TRADE DOLLARS 1873-1885

This coin was issued for circulation in the Orient to compete with the Mexican peso. It contains 420 grains of .900 fine silver; the edge is reeded. In 1887 a law was passed authorizing the Treasury to redeem all trade dollars that were not mutilated. Proofs dated 1878 through 1885 were made for collecting purposes only.

The design is by William Barber, who also engraved the 20c piece. Mint marks are in the field below the eagle.

VERY GOOD—*About half of mottoes IN GOD WE TRUST and E PLURIBUS UNUM will show. Rim on both sides well defined.*
FINE—*Mottoes and LIBERTY readable but worn.*
EXTRA FINE—*Mottoes and LIBERTY are sharp. Only slight wear on rims.*

Date	Thousands Minted	Avg. Dealers Pay V. Good	Fine	Average Retail Prices V. Good	Fine	Ex. Fine
1873	398	$30.00	$40.00	$50.00	$60.00	$125.00
1873CC	125	35.00	45.00	55.00	70.00	150.00
1873S	703	30.00	40.00	52.50	62.50	125.00
1874	988	30.00	40.00	50.00	60.00	110.00
1874CC	1,373	35.00	45.00	55.00	65.00	130.00
1874S	2,549	30.00	40.00	50.00	60.00	110.00
1875	219	35.00	45.00	60.00	75.00	200.00
1875CC	1,574	35.00	45.00	55.00	65.00	150.00
1875S	4,487	30.00	40.00	50.00	60.00	110.00
1876	456	30.00	40.00	50.00	60.00	110.00
1876CC	509	35.00	45.00	55.00	65.00	150.00
1876S	5,227	30.00	40.00	50.00	60.00	110.00
1877	3,040	30.00	40.00	50.00	60.00	110.00
1877CC	534	35.00	45.00	55.00	70.00	165.00
1877S	9,519	30.00	40.00	50.00	60.00	110.00
1878	0.9	Rare				
1878CC	97	65.00	125.00	145.00	200.00	500.00
1878S	4,162	30.00	40.00	50.00	60.00	110.00
1879 thru 1885		Rare				

SILVER DOLLARS
Liberty Head or Morgan Type 1878-1921

All silver dollars are worth a premium for their silver content. Mint marks on reverse, below wreath.

VERY FINE—*Two-thirds of hairlines from top of forehead to ear must show. Ear well defined. Feathers on eagle's breast worn at center.*
EXTRA FINE—*All hairlines strong and ear bold. Eagle's feathers all plain but slight wear on breast and wing tips.*

Date	Millions Minted	Avg. Dealers Pay V. Fine	Ex. Fine	Average Retail Prices V. Fine	Ex. Fine	Unc.
1878	11	*$11.00*	*$13.00*	*$15.00*	$18.00	$63.00
1878CC	2	14.00	20.00	30.00	40.00	125.00
1878S	10	*11.00*	*13.00*	*15.00*	18.00	50.00
1879	15	*11.00*	*13.00*	*15.00*	18.00	55.00
1879CC	0.8	45.00	125.00	75.00	235.00	1,150
1879O	3	*11.00*	*13.00*	*15.00*	20.00	75.00
1879S	9	*11.00*	*13.00*	*15.00*	18.00	50.00
1880	12	*11.00*	*13.00*	*15.00*	18.00	50.00
1880CC	0.6	30.00	37.50	55.00	90.00	250.00
1880O	5	*11.00*	*13.00*	*15.00*	20.00	100.00
1880S	9	*11.00*	*13.00*	*15.00*	18.00	50.00
1881	9	*11.00*	*13.00*	*15.00*	18.00	50.00
1881CC	0.3	40.00	55.00	75.00	100.00	250.00
1881O	6	*11.00*	*13.00*	*15.00*	18.00	55.00
1881S	11	*11.00*	*13.00*	*15.00*	18.00	50.00
1882	11	*11.00*	*13.00*	*15.00*	18.00	50.00
1882CC	1	14.00	17.50	33.00	40.00	100.00
1882O	6	*11.00*	*13.00*	*15.00*	18.00	55.00
1882S	9	*11.00*	*13.00*	*15.00*	18.00	50.00
1883	12	*11.00*	*13.00*	*15.00*	18.00	50.00
1883CC	1	15.00	18.00	33.00	40.00	95.00
1883O	9	*11.00*	*13.00*	*15.00*	17.00	35.00
1883S	6	13.00	17.00	20.00	40.00	550.00
1884	14	*11.00*	*13.00*	*15.00*	20.00	90.00
1884CC	1	17.50	20.00	37.50	45.00	95.00

SILVER DOLLARS

Date	Millions Minted	Avg. Dealers Pay V. Fine	Ex. Fine	Average Retail Prices V. Fine	Ex. Fine	Unc.
1884O	10	$11.00	$13.00	$15.00	$18.00	$35.00
1884S	3	11.00	15.00	23.00	30.00	1,400
1885	18	11.00	13.00	15.00	18.00	35.00
1885CC	0.2	65.00	75.00	120.00	150.00	245.00
1885O	9	11.00	13.00	15.00	18.00	35.00
1885S	1	11.00	15.00	15.00	30.00	200.00
1886	20	11.00	13.00	15.00	18.00	35.00
1886O	11	11.00	13.00	15.00	20.00	575.00
1886S	0.8	15.00	20.00	27.00	35.00	275.00
1887	20	11.00	13.00	15.00	18.00	35.00
1887O	12	11.00	13.00	15.00	18.00	60.00
1887S	2	11.00	13.00	24.00	25.00	145.00
1888	19	11.00	13.00	15.00	18.00	40.00
1888O	12	11.00	13.00	15.00	18.00	50.00
1888S	0.7	15.00	20.00	30.00	40.00	300.00
1889	22	11.00	13.00	15.00	18.00	40.00
1889CC	0.4	140.00	300.00	220.00	450.00	6,500
1889O	12	11.00	13.00	15.00	18.00	150.00
1889S	0.7	14.00	17.50	27.00	33.00	175.00
1890	17	11.00	13.00	15.00	18.00	45.00
1890CC	2	15.00	20.00	33.00	40.00	225.00
1890O	11	11.00	13.00	15.00	18.00	90.00
1890S	8	11.00	13.00	15.00	18.00	85.00
1891	9	11.00	13.00	15.00	18.00	150.00
1891CC	2	15.00	20.00	33.00	45.00	200.00
1891O	8	11.00	13.00	15.00	20.00	175.00
1891S	5	11.00	13.00	15.00	20.00	85.00
1892	1	13.00	15.00	25.00	30.00	200.00
1892CC	1	24.00	50.00	45.00	70.00	400.00
1892O	3	11.00	15.00	23.00	30.00	275.00
1892S	1	18.00	75.00	35.00	125.00	6,000
1893	0.4	22.50	40.00	45.00	65.00	625.00
1893CC	0.7	50.00	160.00	80.00	225.00	1,250
1893O	0.3	40.00	85.00	80.00	165.00	1,400
1893S	0.1	800.00	1,600	1,200	3,000	26,500
1894	0.1	175.00	250.00	285.00	395.00	1,650
1894O	2	14.00	18.00	27.00	35.00	650.00
1894S	1	18.00	40.00	35.00	75.00	550.00
1895	0.01	Rare				
1895O	0.5	50.00	100.00	80.00	195.00	3,500
1895S	0.4	80.00	225.00	140.00	425.00	2,000
1896	10	11.00	13.00	15.00	18.00	42.00
1896O	5	11.00	13.00	15.00	20.00	900.00
1896S	5	17.00	40.00	35.00	80.00	1,000
1897	3	11.00	13.00	15.00	18.00	50.00
1897O	4	11.00	13.00	15.00	18.00	600.00
1897S	6	11.00	13.00	15.00	18.00	95.00
1898	6	11.00	13.00	15.00	18.00	50.00
1898O	4	11.00	13.00	15.00	18.00	40.00
1898S	4	11.00	15.00	24.00	28.00	350.00

SILVER DOLLARS

Date	Millions Minted	Avg. Dealers Pay		Average Retail Prices		
		V. Fine	Ex. Fine	V. Fine	Ex. Fine	Unc.
1899	0.3	$20.00	$25.00	$40.00	$45.00	$135.00
1899O	12	*11.00*	*13.00*	*15.00*	18.00	40.00
1899S	3	*11.00*	16.50	28.00	35.00	475.00
1900	9	*11.00*	*13.00*	*15.00*	18.00	42.00
1900O	13	*11.00*	*13.00*	*15.00*	18.00	42.00
1900S	4	*11.00*	16.00	25.00	30.00	300.00
1901	7	15.00	25.00	25.00	45.00	1,250
1901O	13	*11.00*	*13.00*	*15.00*	18.00	45.00
1901S	2	13.00	27.00	28.00	45.00	500.00
1902	8	*11.00*	*13.00*	*15.00*	18.00	85.00
1902O	9	*11.00*	*13.00*	*15.00*	18.00	40.00
1902S	2	25.00	40.00	45.00	75.00	550.00
1903	5	*11.00*	*13.00*	*15.00*	20.00	85.00
1903O	4	80.00	100.00	175.00	200.00	350.00
1903S	1	19.00	85.00	50.00	200.00	3,000
1904	3	*11.00*	*13.00*	16.00	20.00	200.00
1904O	4	*11.00*	*13.00*	*15.00*	18.00	35.00
1904S	2	15.00	60.00	30.00	150.00	1,700
1921	45	*10.00*	*11.00*	*14.00*	16.00	25.00
1921D	20	*10.00*	*11.00*	*15.00*	18.00	40.00
1921S	22	*10.00*	*11.00*	*15.00*	18.00	65.00

Peace Type 1921-1935

This dollar, which commemorates the end of World War I, was designed by Anthony De Francisci. His monogram is located above the date. Mint marks are on the reverse, left of eagle's wing tip. Last coined for circulation in 1935, silver dollars are no longer found in circulation and all are worth a premium for their silver content.

V. FINE—Hair over eye well worn. Some strands over ear well defined. Some eagle feathers on top and outside edge of right wing will show.

EX. FINE—Hairlines over brow and ear are strong though slightly worn. Outside wing feathers at right and those at top are visible but faint.

SILVER DOLLARS

Date	Millions Minted	Avg. Dealers Pay		Average Retail Prices		
		V. Fine	Ex. Fine	V. Fine	Ex. Fine	Unc.
1921	1	$20.00	$25.00	$40.00	$70.00	$450.00
1922	52	*10.00*	*11.00*	*15.00*	16.00	27.00
1922D	15	*10.00*	*11.00*	*15.00*	17.00	50.00
1922S	17	*10.00*	*11.00*	*15.00*	17.00	60.00
1923	31	*10.00*	*11.00*	*15.00*	16.00	27.00
1923D	7	*10.00*	*11.00*	*15.00*	17.00	55.00
1923S	19	*10.00*	*11.00*	*15.00*	17.00	60.00
1924	12	*10.00*	*11.00*	*15.00*	17.00	42.00
1924S	2	*10.00*	*11.00*	*15.00*	22.00	265.00
1925	10	*10.00*	*11.00*	*15.00*	17.00	40.00
1925S	2	*10.00*	*11.00*	*15.00*	20.00	200.00
1926	2	*10.00*	*11.00*	*15.00*	18.00	60.00
1926D	2	*10.00*	*11.00*	*15.00*	20.00	160.00
1926S	7	*10.00*	*11.00*	*15.00*	18.00	75.00
1927	0.8	14.00	16.00	16.00	30.00	150.00
1927D	1	14.00	16.00	17.00	35.00	375.00
1927S	0.9	14.00	16.00	20.00	35.00	400.00
1928	0.4	95.00	125.00	165.00	195.00	375.00
1928S	2	*13.00*	14.00	18.00	30.00	300.00
1934	1	14.00	16.00	20.00	32.00	145.00
1934D	2	14.00	16.00	17.00	29.00	225.00
1934S	1	15.00	75.00	25.00	135.00	2,750
1935	2	*13.00*	14.00	17.00	26.00	100.00
1935S	2	14.00	15.00	17.00	25.00	275.00

Mint mark location on reverse below ONE

Values shown in these listings are averages of prices quoted by dealers throughout the country. The publisher of this book does not buy, sell, or appraise coins.

SILVER DOLLARS
EISENHOWER DOLLARS 1971-1978

Intended to honor both the late President Dwight D. Eisenhower and first landing of man on the moon, the reverse is an adaptation of the official Apollo 11 insignia. Collectors' coins were struck in 40% silver composition, circulation issue in copper-nickel. Mint mark above date.

Date	Millions Minted	Avg. Dealers Pay Unc.	Proof	Average Retail Prices Unc.	Proof
1971 clad	48	$1.00		$2.25	
1971D clad	69	1.00		2.50	
1971S silver	11	3.00	$5.00	6.00	$9.00
1972 clad	76	1.00		2.25	
1972D clad	93	1.00		2.25	
1972S silver	4	11.00	14.00	13.00	19.50
1973 clad	2	12.50		15.00	
1973D clad	2	12.50		15.00	
1973S clad	3		3.50		6.00
1973S silver	2	12.00	70.00	14.50	90.00
1974 clad	27	1.00		2.25	
1974D clad	45	1.00		2.25	
1974S clad	3		3.50		6.00
1974S silver	1	11.00	17.00	13.00	23.00
1977 clad	13	1.00		2.50	
1977D clad	33	1.00		2.25	
1977S clad	3		2.50		4.50
1978 clad	26	1.00		2.25	
1978D clad	23	1.00		2.25	
1978S clad	3		9.00		12.00

BICENTENNIAL COINAGE DATED 1776-1976

The national significance of the Bicentennial of the United States was highlighted with the adoption of new reverse designs for the quarter, half dollar and dollar. Nearly a thousand entries were submitted after the Treasury announced in October of 1973 that an open contest was to be held for the selection of the new designs. After the field was narrowed down to twelve semifinalists, the judges chose the rendition

BICENTENNIAL DOLLARS

of the Liberty Bell superimposed on the moon to appear on the dollar coins. This design was the work of Dennis R. Williams. The obverse remained unchanged except for the dual date 1776-1976, which appeared on all dollars made during 1975 and 1976. In addition to being included in the various offerings of proof and uncirculated coins made by the Mint, they were also struck at Philadelphia and Denver for circulation.

Date	Millions Minted	Avg. Dealers Pay Unc.	Proof	Average Retail Prices Unc.	Proof
1976	117	$1.00		$2.25	
1976D	103	1.00		2.25	
1976S	7		$3.00		$4.50
1976S silver	7	8.00	9.50	10.00	12.50

ANTHONY DOLLARS 1979-1981

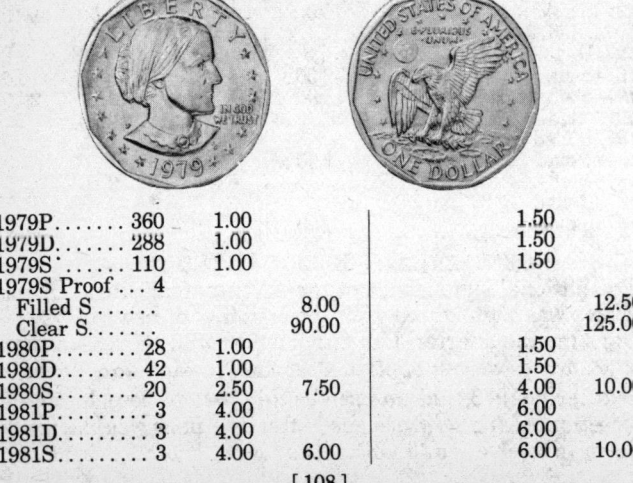

1979P	360	1.00		1.50	
1979D	288	1.00		1.50	
1979S	110	1.00		1.50	
1979S Proof	4				
Filled S			8.00		12.50
Clear S			90.00		125.00
1980P	28	1.00		1.50	
1980D	42	1.00		1.50	
1980S	20	2.50	7.50	4.00	10.00
1981P	3	4.00		6.00	
1981D	3	4.00		6.00	
1981S	3	4.00	6.00	6.00	10.00

GOLD COINS 1795-1933

Gold coins were made and used in the United States from 1795 to 1933. Most of these coins are scarce today, as many of them were melted under the Gold Redemption Act of 1933. It is legal to own gold coins, but they are no longer legal tender.

The standard gold unit authorized in the act of April 2, 1792 was the *Eagle* or $10.00 gold piece. Weight and fineness were established at 270 grains, 916 2/3 thousandths. Half and quarter eagles were based on the same standard. In 1837 this was changed to 258 grains, .900 fine, and in 1849 gold dollars and double eagles were authorized, based on this standard. The $3.00 gold piece was authorized in 1854. The designs used for the various denominations follow a general pattern.

Minor varieties of early gold coins exist and some of these are worth a premium. Several overdates are known. This series includes some of the rarest and most valuable United States coins.

Mint marks are located on the reverse below the eagle on most gold coins.

GOLD DOLLARS 1849-1889
Liberty Head Type 1849-1854

***FINE**—Full LIBERTY but knobs over coronet partially worn.*
***VERY FINE**—LIBERTY on headband complete and readable. Knobs on coronet are defined.*
***EX. FINE**—Little wear on hair, knobs on coronet must be bold.*

Date	Thousands Minted	Average Dealers Pay	Average Retail Prices		
			Fine	V. Fine	Ex. Fine
1849	689	$125.00	$150.00	$200.00	$250.00
1849C	12	200.00	250.00	300.00	500.00
1849D	22	225.00	225.00	275.00	475.00
1849O	215	125.00	150.00	200.00	250.00
1850	482	125.00	150.00	200.00	250.00
1850C	7	250.00	300.00	350.00	550.00
1850D	8	275.00	275.00	325.00	525.00
1850O	14	150.00	200.00	250.00	400.00

GOLD DOLLARS

Date	Thousands Minted	Average Dealers Pay	Average Retail Prices		
			Fine	V. Fine	Ex. Fine
1851	3,318	$150.00	$150.00	$200.00	$250.00
1851C	41	200.00	250.00	300.00	450.00
1851D	10	250.00	275.00	325.00	525.00
1851O	290	150.00	150.00	200.00	250.00
1852	2,045	150.00	150.00	200.00	250.00
1852C	9	200.00	225.00	275.00	450.00
1852D	6	200.00	250.00	300.00	500.00
1852O	140	150.00	150.00	200.00	250.00
1853	4,076	150.00	150.00	200.00	250.00
1853C	12	175.00	225.00	275.00	450.00
1853D	7	225.00	250.00	300.00	500.00
1853O	290	150.00	150.00	200.00	250.00
1854	737	150.00	150.00	200.00	250.00
1854D	3	375.00	375.00	450.00	700.00
1854S	15	200.00	225.00	275.00	450.00

Indian Head Type 1854-1856
Small head

FINE—Tips of feather curls on headdress partially worn away.
VERY FINE—Feather curl tips outlined but details worn.
EX. FINE—Slight wear on headdress feather curls.

1854	903	200.00	250.00	350.00	700.00
1855	758	200.00	250.00	350.00	700.00
1855C	10	485.00	550.00	600.00	1,000
1855D	2	1,500	2,000	2,500	4,000
1855O	55	400.00	450.00	500.00	950.00
1856S	25	375.00	425.00	475.00	900.00

Gold coins are usually found in Very Fine or better condition, as few of them received wide circulation. The values quoted in this guide are average buying prices for coins with minimum wear, nicks or scratches. Damaged coins have no collector value. See page 4.

GOLD DOLLARS
Indian Head Type 1856-1889
Large head

FINE—Full LIBERTY in headband. Beads partially worn. Curled feathers worn flat.
VERY FINE—Curled feathers have slight detail. Details worn smooth at eyebrow, hair below headdress and behind ear and bottom curl.
EX. FINE—Trace of wear above and right of eye and on curled feathers.

Date	Thousands Minted	Average Dealers Pay	Average Retail Prices		
			Fine	V. Fine	Ex. Fine
1856	1,763	$125.00	$150.00	$175.00	$200.00
1856D	1	1,750	2,000	2,500	4,250
1857	775	125.00	150.00	175.00	200.00
1857C	13	350.00	350.00	425.00	525.00
1857D	4	425.00	400.00	500.00	800.00
1857S	10	175.00	200.00	250.00	350.00
1858	118	125.00	150.00	175.00	200.00
1858D	3	450.00	550.00	650.00	900.00
1858S	10	175.00	200.00	250.00	350.00
1859	168	125.00	150.00	175.00	200.00
1859C	5	300.00	325.00	400.00	600.00
1859D	5	350.00	375.00	450.00	750.00
1859S	15	200.00	200.00	250.00	350.00
1860	37	125.00	150.00	175.00	200.00
1860D	2	1,000	1,500	2,200	4,500
1860S	13	200.00	200.00	250.00	350.00
1861	527	125.00	150.00	175.00	200.00
1861D		3,500	2,750	4,500	7,000
1862	1,361	125.00	150.00	175.00	200.00
1863	6	200.00	275.00	350.00	550.00
1864	6	200.00	250.00	325.00	500.00
1865	4	200.00	250.00	325.00	500.00
1866	7	150.00	200.00	250.00	475.00
1867	5	170.00	250.00	300.00	500.00
1868	11	135.00	175.00	225.00	450.00
1869	6	150.00	200.00	250.00	475.00
1870	6	150.00	200.00	250.00	475.00
1870S	3	325.00	400.00	500.00	900.00
1871	4	150.00	200.00	250.00	450.00
1872	4	150.00	200.00	250.00	450.00

GOLD DOLLARS

Date	Thousands Minted	Average Dealers Pay	Average Retail Prices		
			Fine	V. Fine	Ex. Fine
1873	125	$125.00	$125.00	$175.00	$200.00
1874	199	125.00	125.00	175.00	200.00
1875	0.4	1,350	1,500	2,000	3,000
1876	3	150.00	175.00	225.00	300.00
1877	4	175.00	200.00	250.00	275.00
1878	3	175.00	200.00	250.00	275.00
1879	3	175.00	200.00	250.00	275.00
1880	2	175.00	200.00	250.00	275.00
1881	8	150.00	150.00	200.00	250.00
1882	5	150.00	150.00	200.00	250.00
1883	11	125.00	150.00	200.00	250.00
1884	6	150.00	150.00	200.00	250.00
1885	12	125.00	150.00	200.00	250.00
1886	6	150.00	150.00	200.00	250.00
1887	9	125.00	150.00	200.00	250.00
1888	17	125.00	150.00	200.00	250.00
1889	31	125.00	150.00	200.00	250.00

Gold, the earliest known and most beautiful of all metallic substances, has been and remains of the greatest commercial consequence. Of the precious metals, gold particularly has for ages been the chief material used for coins.

Gold is common to most nations as a standard for measurement of all other values. In our own country paper currency and token coins now serve exclusively as money. Gold continues to serve as the yardstick of money values, although it is no longer used for actual coinage.

QUARTER EAGLES ($2.50 Gold Pieces) 1796-1929

Capped Bust to Right 1796-1807

FINE—Hair worn smooth on high spots. E. PLURIBUS UNUM weak but readable.
VERY FINE—Some wear on high spots.
EX. FINE—Slight wear on high spots.

QUARTER EAGLES

Date	Thousands Minted	Average Dealers Pay	Average Retail Prices		
			Fine	V. Fine	Ex. Fine
1796 No stars	1	$6,000	$9,000	$13,000	$18,000

1796 Stars	0.4	5,000	7,000	12,000	16,000
1797	0.4	3,250	6,000	9,000	13,000
1798	1	2,100	4,500	6,000	7,500
1802	3	1,200	2,500	4,000	6,000
1804	3	1,200	2,500	4,000	6,000
1805	2	1,200	2,500	4,000	6,000
1806	2	1,200	2,500	4,000	6,000
1807	7	1,000	2,000	3,000	5,000

Capped Bust to Left 1808-1834

FINE—E. PLURIBUS UNUM and LIBERTY on headband readable but weak.
VERY FINE—Motto and LIBERTY clear.
EX. FINE—Motto and LIBERTY sharp. Liberty's hair only slightly worn.

1808	3	4,500	7,500	12,000	22,500
1821 Reduced size	6	1,000	2,500	4,000	6,000
1824	3	1,000	2,500	4,000	6,000
1825	4	1,000	2,500	4,000	6,000
1826	0.8	1,500	5,000	7,500	10,000
1827	3	1,200	3,000	4,500	6,000
1829	3	950.00	2,500	3,500	7,000
1830	5	950.00	1,750	2,500	4,500
1831	5	950.00	1,750	2,500	4,500
1832	4	950.00	1,750	2,500	4,500
1833	4	950.00	1,750	2,500	4,500
1834	4	3,000	4,500	7,500	12,000

QUARTER EAGLES
Liberty Without Cap 1834-1839

FINE—*LIBERTY readable and complete. Curl below ear outlined but no detail.*
VERY FINE—*LIBERTY plain. Hair curl has detail.*
EX. FINE—*Slight wear on hair at top of head, below L in LIBERTY, top of coronet and on reverse, upper wings and neck of eagle.*

Date	Thousands Minted	Average Dealers Pay	Average Retail Prices		
			Fine	V. Fine	Ex. Fine
1834	112	$240.00	$275.00	$350.00	$475.00
1835	131	240.00	275.00	350.00	475.00
1836	548	240.00	275.00	350.00	475.00
1837	45	240.00	275.00	375.00	500.00
1838	47	240.00	275.00	375.00	500.00
1838C	8	275.00	375.00	550.00	1,250
1839	27	240.00	275.00	375.00	500.00
1839C	18	300.00	350.00	500.00	1,000
1839D	14	300.00	350.00	500.00	1,100
1839O	18	240.00	275.00	375.00	600.00

Coronet Type 1840-1907

1840	19	160.00	190.00	275.00	350.00
1840C	13	275.00	325.00	450.00	700.00
1840D	4	300.00	350.00	475.00	1,000
1840O	34	160.00	190.00	275.00	325.00
1841		Rare			
1841C	10	275.00	325.00	425.00	700.00
1841D	4	300.00	350.00	450.00	700.00

QUARTER EAGLES

Date	Thousands Minted	Average Dealers Pay	Average Retail Prices		
			Fine	V. Fine	Ex. Fine
1842	3	$350.00	$400.00	$500.00	$800.00
1842C	7	275.00	325.00	450.00	700.00
1842D	5	350.00	400.00	500.00	800.00
1842O	20	160.00	200.00	275.00	350.00
1843	101	160.00	200.00	275.00	325.00
1843C	26	250.00	325.00	425.00	600.00
1843D	36	250.00	325.00	425.00	600.00
1843O	364	150.00	175.00	225.00	275.00
1844	7	225.00	200.00	275.00	375.00
1844C	12	250.00	275.00	325.00	425.00
1844D	17	250.00	275.00	325.00	425.00
1845	91	150.00	150.00	175.00	225.00
1845D	19	250.00	275.00	325.00	425.00
1845O	4	300.00	325.00	400.00	500.00
1846	22	150.00	150.00	175.00	225.00
1846C	5	325.00	300.00	375.00	650.00
1846D	19	250.00	275.00	325.00	425.00
1846O	62	150.00	150.00	175.00	225.00
1847	30	150.00	150.00	175.00	225.00
1847C	23	200.00	250.00	300.00	400.00
1847D	16	200.00	250.00	300.00	400.00
1847O	124	150.00	150.00	175.00	225.00
1848	7	450.00	325.00	425.00	650.00

CAL. Above Eagle on Reverse

Date	Thousands Minted	Average Dealers Pay	Fine	V. Fine	Ex. Fine
1848 CAL. over eagle	1	3,000	3,000	4,500	7,000
1848C	17	275.00	275.00	350.00	475.00
1848D	14	275.00	325.00	400.00	575.00
1849	23	150.00	150.00	200.00	275.00
1849C	10	225.00	275.00	325.00	450.00
1849D	11	225.00	275.00	350.00	550.00
1850	253	150.00	150.00	175.00	225.00
1850C	9	200.00	275.00	325.00	450.00
1850D	12	200.00	275.00	325.00	450.00
1850O	84	150.00	150.00	175.00	225.00
1851	1,373	150.00	150.00	175.00	225.00

QUARTER EAGLES

Date	Thousands Minted	Average Dealers Pay	Average Retail Prices		
			Fine	V. Fine	Ex. Fine
1851C	15	$200.00	$200.00	$250.00	$400.00
1851D	11	200.00	200.00	250.00	400.00
1851O	148	125.00	150.00	175.00	250.00
1852	1,160	125.00	150.00	175.00	250.00
1852C	10	225.00	225.00	275.00	450.00
1852D	4	300.00	300.00	375.00	550.00
1852O	140	125.00	150.00	175.00	250.00
1853	1,405	125.00	150.00	175.00	250.00
1853D	3	350.00	400.00	500.00	800.00
1854	596	125.00	150.00	175.00	250.00
1854C	7	225.00	225.00	275.00	450.00
1854D	2	1,100	1,250	1,750	2,750
1854O	153	125.00	150.00	175.00	250.00
1854S	0.2	Rare			
1855	235	125.00	150.00	175.00	250.00
1855C	4	350.00	450.00	600.00	900.00
1855D	1	650.00	1,000	1,400	2,200
1856	384	125.00	150.00	175.00	250.00
1856C	8	250.00	250.00	300.00	400.00
1856D	0.9	1,150	1,750	2,200	4,000
1856O	21	125.00	150.00	175.00	250.00
1856S	71	125.00	150.00	175.00	250.00
1857	214	125.00	150.00	175.00	250.00
1857D	2	325.00	325.00	400.00	600.00
1857O	34	125.00	150.00	175.00	250.00
1857S	69	125.00	150.00	175.00	250.00
1858	47	125.00	150.00	175.00	250.00
1858C	9	250.00	250.00	300.00	400.00
1859	39	125.00	150.00	175.00	250.00
1859D	2	325.00	325.00	400.00	325.00
1859S	15	125.00	150.00	175.00	250.00
1860	23	125.00	150.00	175.00	250.00
1860C	7	250.00	250.00	300.00	450.00
1860S	36	125.00	150.00	175.00	250.00
1861	1,284	125.00	150.00	175.00	250.00
1861S	24	125.00	150.00	175.00	250.00
1862	99	125.00	150.00	175.00	250.00
1862S	8	125.00	150.00	175.00	250.00
1863	0.03	Rare			
1863S	11	125.00	150.00	175.00	250.00
1864	3	325.00	325.00	450.00	600.00
1865	2	325.00	325.00	450.00	600.00
1865S	23	125.00	150.00	175.00	250.00
1866	3	250.00	250.00	300.00	400.00
1866S	39	125.00	150.00	175.00	250.00
1867	3	250.00	250.00	300.00	400.00
1867S	28	125.00	150.00	175.00	250.00
1868	4	250.00	250.00	300.00	400.00
1868S	34	125.00	150.00	175.00	250.00

QUARTER EAGLES

Date	Thousands Minted	Average Dealers Pay	Average Retail Prices		
			Fine	V. Fine	Ex. Fine
1869	4	$140.00	$160.00	$200.00	$300.00
1869S	30	125.00	150.00	175.00	250.00
1870	5	140.00	160.00	200.00	300.00
1870S	16	125.00	150.00	175.00	250.00
1871	5	140.00	160.00	200.00	300.00
1871S	22	125.00	150.00	175.00	250.00
1872	3	200.00	200.00	300.00	400.00
1872S	18	125.00	150.00	175.00	250.00
1873	178	125.00	150.00	175.00	225.00
1873S	27	125.00	150.00	175.00	250.00
1874	4	200.00	200.00	250.00	350.00
1875	0.4	1,100	1,250	1,750	3,500
1875S	12	125.00	150.00	175.00	250.00
1876	4	140.00	160.00	200.00	300.00
1876S	5	125.00	150.00	175.00	250.00
1877	2	350.00	375.00	450.00	650.00
1877S	35	125.00	150.00	175.00	225.00
1878	286	125.00	150.00	175.00	225.00
1878S	178	125.00	150.00	175.00	225.00
1879	89	125.00	150.00	175.00	225.00
1879S	44	125.00	150.00	175.00	225.00
1880	3	140.00	160.00	200.00	275.00
1881	0.7	450.00	450.00	600.00	900.00
1882	4	140.00	160.00	200.00	275.00
1883	2	200.00	200.00	250.00	325.00
1884	2	200.00	200.00	250.00	325.00
1885	0.9	450.00	450.00	600.00	900.00
1886	4	140.00	160.00	200.00	275.00
1887	6	125.00	150.00	175.00	250.00
1888	16	125.00	150.00	175.00	225.00
1889	18	125.00	150.00	175.00	225.00
1890	9	125.00	150.00	175.00	250.00
1891	11	125.00	150.00	175.00	225.00
1892	3	200.00	200.00	250.00	300.00
1893	30	125.00	150.00	175.00	225.00
1894	4	150.00	160.00	200.00	275.00
1895	6	125.00	150.00	175.00	250.00
1896	19	125.00	150.00	175.00	225.00
1897	30	125.00	150.00	175.00	225.00
1898	24	125.00	150.00	175.00	225.00
1899	27	125.00	150.00	175.00	225.00
1900	67	125.00	150.00	175.00	225.00
1901	91	125.00	150.00	175.00	225.00
1902	134	125.00	150.00	175.00	225.00
1903	201	125.00	150.00	175.00	225.00
1904	161	125.00	150.00	175.00	225.00
1905	218	125.00	150.00	175.00	225.00
1906	176	125.00	150.00	175.00	225.00
1907	336	125.00	150.00	175.00	225.00

QUARTER EAGLES
Indian Head Type 1908-1929

FINE—*Knot in haircord must show, small feathers on top of head will be faint.*
VERY FINE—*Haircord knot distinct. Feathers at top of head clear. Cheekbone worn.*
EXTRA FINE—*Cheekbone, war bonnet and headband feathers slightly worn.*

Date	Thousands Minted	Average Dealers Pay	Average Retail Prices		
			Fine	V. Fine	Ex. Fine
1908	565	$125.00	$120.00	$150.00	$175.00
1909	442	125.00	120.00	150.00	175.00
1910	493	125.00	120.00	150.00	175.00
1911	704	125.00	120.00	150.00	175.00
1911D	56	350.00	500.00	750.00	1,500
1912	616	125.00	120.00	150.00	175.00
1913	722	125.00	120.00	150.00	175.00
1914	240	125.00	120.00	150.00	175.00
1914D	448	125.00	120.00	150.00	175.00
1915	606	125.00	120.00	150.00	175.00
1925D	578	125.00	120.00	150.00	175.00
1926	446	125.00	120.00	150.00	175.00
1927	388	125.00	120.00	150.00	175.00
1928	416	125.00	120.00	150.00	175.00
1929	532	125.00	120.00	150.00	175.00

THREE DOLLAR GOLD PIECES 1854-1889

FINE—*Details of curled feathers missing. Beads partly worn, but LIBERTY plain.*
VERY FINE—*Eyebrow, hair about forehead and ear and bottom curl are worn smooth. Curled feather-ends have faint details showing.*
EX. FINE—*Slight wear above and to right of eye, and tops of curled feathers.*

THREE DOLLAR GOLD PIECES

Date	Thousands Minted	Average Dealers Pay	Average Retail Prices		
			Fine	V. Fine	Ex. Fine
1854	139	$350.00	$500.00	$650.00	$900.00
1854D	1	1,500	2,500	4,500	8,500
1854O	24	350.00	500.00	650.00	900.00
1855	51	350.00	500.00	650.00	900.00
1855S	7	400.00	550.00	750.00	1,200
1856	26	350.00	500.00	650.00	900.00
1856S	35	350.00	500.00	725.00	1,100
1857	21	350.00	500.00	650.00	900.00
1857S	14	350.00	500.00	750.00	1,200
1858	2	425.00	600.00	800.00	1,300
1859	16	350.00	500.00	650.00	900.00
1860	7	350.00	500.00	725.00	1,100
1860S	7	350.00	500.00	800.00	1,300
1861	6	350.00	500.00	725.00	1,100
1862	6	350.00	500.00	725.00	1,100
1863	5	350.00	500.00	775.00	1,100
1864	3	350.00	500.00	775.00	1,100
1865	1	500.00	650.00	950.00	1,400
1866	4	350.00	500.00	775.00	1,100
1867	3	350.00	500.00	775.00	1,100
1868	5	350.00	500.00	775.00	1,100
1869	3	350.00	500.00	775.00	1,100
1870	4	350.00	500.00	775.00	1,100
1870S		Rare			
1871	1	350.00	500.00	850.00	1,200
1872	2	350.00	500.00	775.00	1,100
1873		Rare			
1874	42	350.00	500.00	650.00	900.00
1875	0.02	Rare			
1876	0.05	Rare			
1877	1	475.00	700.00	950.00	1,750
1878	82	350.00	500.00	650.00	900.00
1879	3	350.00	500.00	775.00	1,100
1880	1	350.00	500.00	850.00	1,200
1881	0.5	500.00	750.00	1,000	1,700
1882	2	350.00	500.00	775.00	1,100
1883	1	350.00	500.00	850.00	1,200
1884	1	350.00	500.00	850.00	1,200
1885	1	425.00	600.00	900.00	1,300
1886	1	350.00	500.00	775.00	1,100
1887	6	350.00	500.00	700.00	1,000
1888	5	350.00	500.00	700.00	1,000
1889	2	350.00	500.00	700.00	1,000

Values shown in these listings are averages of prices quoted by dealers throughout the country. The publisher of this book does not buy, sell, or appraise coins.

HALF EAGLES ($5.00 Gold Pieces) 1795-1929
Capped Bust to Right, Small Eagle 1795-1798

FINE—*Hair worn smooth but with distinct outline. After 1797 E PLURIBUS UNUM is faint but readable.*
VERY FINE—*Slight to noticeable wear on high spots such as hair, turban, eagle's head and wings.*
EX. FINE—*Slight wear on hair and cheek.*

Date	Thousands Minted	Average Dealers Pay	Average Retail Prices		
			Fine	V. Fine	Ex. Fine
1795 Small eagle	9	$2,250	$3,500	$5,250	$8,000
1796 Small eagle	6	2,500	4,500	6,000	10,000
1797 Small eagle	4	3,500	6,000	8,500	13,000
1798 Small eagle		Rare			

Capped Bust to Right, Large Eagle 1795-1807

1795 Large eagle		3,250	5,500	8,500	14,000
1797 Large eagle		2,600	5,000	7,500	12,000
1798 Large eagle	25	650.00	1,000	2,000	3,000
1799	7	650.00	1,000	2,000	3,000
1800	38	650.00	1,000	2,000	3,000
1802	53	650.00	1,000	2,000	3,000
1803	34	650.00	1,000	2,000	3,000
1804	30	650.00	1,000	2,000	3,000
1805	33	650.00	1,000	2,000	3,000
1806	64	650.00	1,000	2,000	3,000
1807	32	650.00	1,000	2,000	3,000

HALF EAGLES

Capped Bust to Left 1807-1838
Round cap, smaller eagle, Value 5D. used for first time

FINE—LIBERTY readable but partly weak.
VERY FINE—Headband edges slightly worn. LIBERTY is bold.
EX. FINE—Slight wear on high points of hair and curls.

Date	Thousands Minted	Average Dealers Pay	Average Retail Prices		
			Fine	V. Fine	Ex. Fine
1807	52	$700.00	$1,200	$1,700	$2,900
1808	56	600.00	1,000	1,500	2,500
1809	34	600.00	1,000	1,500	2,500
1810	100	600.00	1,000	1,500	2,500
1811	100	600.00	1,000	1,500	2,500
1812	58	600.00	1,000	1,500	2,500

1813	95	650.00	1,100	1,600	2,750
1814	15	750.00	1,400	2,400	3,500
1815	0.6	Rare			
1818	49	700.00	1,200	2,000	3,000
1819	52	Rare			
1820	264	700.00	1,200	2,200	3,500
1821	35	1,600	2,750	5,500	8,000
1822	18	Rare			
1823	14	1,100	1,750	3,000	4,250
1824	17	3,000	5,000	8,500	17,000

HALF EAGLES

Date	Thousands Minted	Average Dealers Pay	Average Retail Prices		
			Fine	V. Fine	Ex. Fine
1825	29	$1,350	$2,500	$4,000	$7,000
1826	18	1,500	2,800	5,000	8,500
1827	25	3,000	5,000	9,000	27,500
1828	28	2,500	4,000	6,000	13,000
1829	57	Rare			
1830	126	1,250	2,200	3,500	5,000
1831	141	1,250	2,200	3,500	5,000
1832	157	2,650	4,500	6,500	9,500
1833	194	1,250	2,200	3,500	5,000
1834	50	1,300	2,200	3,500	5,000

Reduced size, no motto on reverse 1834-1838

1834	657	200.00	250.00	350.00	500.00
1835	372	200.00	250.00	350.00	500.00
1836	553	200.00	250.00	350.00	500.00
1837	207	200.00	250.00	350.00	500.00
1838	287	200.00	250.00	350.00	500.00
1838C	17	400.00	750.00	1,000	1,900
1838D	21	400.00	750.00	1,000	1,900

Coronet Type, Smaller Head, 1839-1908
No motto over eagle 1839-1866

FINE—LIBERTY readable, but partly weak, Neck hair worn, but outlines clear.
VERY FINE—LIBERTY bold. Major lines show in neck hair.
EX. FINE—Hair at neck sharp. Slight wear top of coronet and hair beneath.

HALF EAGLES

Date	Thousands Minted	Average Dealers Pay	Average Retail Prices		
			Fine	V. Fine	Ex. Fine
1839	118	$125.00	$175.00	$200.00	$350.00
1839C	17	240.00	300.00	375.00	600.00
1839D	19	240.00	300.00	375.00	600.00
1840	137	125.00	175.00	200.00	250.00
1840C	19	225.00	300.00	375.00	600.00
1840D	23	225.00	300.00	375.00	600.00
1840O	40	150.00	275.00	325.00	450.00
1841	16	150.00	275.00	325.00	450.00
1841C	21	225.00	325.00	375.00	600.00
1841D	29	225.00	300.00	375.00	600.00
1841O	0.05	Rare			
1842	28	125.00	150.00	175.00	300.00
1842C	27	150.00	275.00	325.00	450.00
1842D	60	150.00	275.00	325.00	450.00
1842O	16	150.00	225.00	275.00	400.00
1843	611	125.00	150.00	175.00	200.00
1843C	44	150.00	275.00	325.00	450.00
1843D	98	150.00	275.00	325.00	450.00
1843O	101	150.00	200.00	250.00	325.00
1844	340	125.00	150.00	175.00	200.00
1844C	24	210.00	300.00	350.00	550.00
1844D	89	150.00	275.00	325.00	450.00
1844O	365	125.00	175.00	225.00	325.00
1845	417	125.00	150.00	175.00	200.00
1845D	91	150.00	275.00	325.00	450.00
1845O	41	125.00	175.00	225.00	325.00
1846	396	125.00	150.00	175.00	200.00
1846C	13	225.00	300.00	375.00	600.00
1846D	80	200.00	275.00	325.00	450.00
1846O	58	125.00	175.00	225.00	325.00
1847	916	125.00	150.00	175.00	200.00
1847C	84	150.00	275.00	325.00	450.00
1847D	64	150.00	275.00	325.00	450.00
1847O	12	150.00	300.00	350.00	500.00
1848	261	125.00	150.00	175.00	200.00
1848C	64	150.00	275.00	325.00	450.00
1848D	47	150.00	275.00	325.00	450.00
1849	133	125.00	150.00	175.00	200.00
1849C	65	150.00	275.00	325.00	450.00
1849D	39	150.00	275.00	325.00	450.00
1850	64	125.00	150.00	175.00	200.00
1850C	64	150.00	275.00	325.00	450.00
1850D	44	150.00	275.00	325.00	450.00
1851	378	125.00	150.00	175.00	200.00
1851C	49	150.00	275.00	325.00	450.00
1851D	63	150.00	275.00	325.00	450.00
1851O	41	125.00	200.00	250.00	375.00
1852	574	125.00	150.00	175.00	200.00
1852C	73	150.00	275.00	325.00	450.00

HALF EAGLES

Date	Thousands Minted	Average Dealers Pay	Average Retail Prices		
			Fine	V. Fine	Ex. Fine
1852D	92	$190.00	$275.00	$325.00	$450.00
1853	306	125.00	150.00	175.00	200.00
1853C	66	190.00	275.00	325.00	450.00
1853D	90	190.00	275.00	325.00	450.00
1854	161	125.00	150.00	175.00	200.00
1854C	39	190.00	275.00	325.00	450.00
1854D	56	190.00	275.00	325.00	450.00
1854O	46	150.00	175.00	225.00	375.00
1854S	0.3	Rare			
1855	117	125.00	150.00	175.00	200.00
1855C	40	190.00	275.00	325.00	450.00
1855D	22	190.00	275.00	325.00	450.00
1855O	11	190.00	275.00	325.00	450.00
1855S	61	125.00	150.00	175.00	250.00
1856	198	125.00	150.00	175.00	200.00
1856C	28	190.00	275.00	325.00	450.00
1856D	20	190.00	275.00	325.00	450.00
1856O	10	240.00	350.00	400.00	650.00
1856S	105	125.00	150.00	175.00	200.00
1857	98	125.00	150.00	175.00	200.00
1857C	31	190.00	275.00	325.00	450.00
1857D	17	190.00	275.00	325.00	450.00
1857O	13	190.00	275.00	325.00	450.00
1857S	87	125.00	150.00	175.00	200.00
1858	15	150.00	175.00	225.00	350.00
1858C	39	190.00	275.00	325.00	450.00
1858D	15	190.00	275.00	325.00	450.00
1858S	19	150.00	175.00	225.00	350.00
1859	17	150.00	175.00	225.00	350.00
1859C	32	190.00	275.00	325.00	450.00
1859D	10	300.00	275.00	375.00	575.00
1859S	13	150.00	175.00	225.00	350.00
1860	20	150.00	175.00	225.00	350.00
1860C	15	190.00	275.00	325.00	450.00
1860D	15	190.00	275.00	325.00	450.00
1860S	21	150.00	175.00	225.00	350.00
1861	688	125.00	150.00	175.00	200.00
1861C	7	700.00	800.00	1,100	1,800
1861D	2	1,950	2,000	2,750	4,500
1861S	18	150.00	175.00	225.00	350.00
1862	4	190.00	200.00	250.00	375.00
1862S	10	225.00	275.00	325.00	525.00
1863	2	260.00	350.00	400.00	750.00
1863S	17	190.00	200.00	250.00	375.00
1864	4	225.00	275.00	325.00	450.00
1864S	4	625.00	650.00	800.00	1,500
1865	1	425.00	550.00	700.00	850.00
1865S	28	190.00	200.00	250.00	375.00
1866S	9	225.00	250.00	300.00	400.00

HALF EAGLES

Motto over eagle 1866-1908

FINE—All letters in motto IN GOD WE TRUST readable.
VERY FINE—Half of hairlines above coronet missing. Hair curls under ear evident, but worn. Motto and its ribbon sharp.
EX. FINE—Slight wear on hair at top of head below L in LIBERTY, top of coronet, and on reverse, upper wings and neck of eagle.

Date	Thousands Minted	Average Dealers Pay	Average Retail Prices		
			Fine	V. Fine	Ex. Fine
1866	7	$200.00	$250.00	$300.00	$450.00
1866S	35	190.00	200.00	250.00	425.00
1867	7	190.00	250.00	300.00	450.00
1867S	29	150.00	175.00	225.00	400.00
1868	6	200.00	250.00	300.00	450.00
1868S	52	150.00	175.00	225.00	400.00
1869	2	300.00	300.00	400.00	600.00
1869S	31	150.00	175.00	200.00	275.00
1870	4	200.00	225.00	275.00	425.00
1870CC	8	850.00	1,000	1,500	2,500
1870S	17	150.00	175.00	200.00	325.00
1871	3	225.00	250.00	300.00	450.00
1871CC	21	280.00	375.00	450.00	650.00
1871S	25	150.00	175.00	200.00	325.00
1872	2	350.00	400.00	500.00	650.00
1872CC	17	350.00	400.00	500.00	650.00
1872S	36	150.00	175.00	200.00	275.00
1873	113	125.00	150.00	175.00	200.00
1873CC	7	325.00	400.00	500.00	850.00
1873S	31	160.00	175.00	200.00	325.00
1874	4	210.00	250.00	300.00	450.00
1874CC	21	210.00	250.00	300.00	450.00
1874S	16	150.00	175.00	200.00	300.00
1875	0.2	Rare			
1875CC	12	280.00	325.00	425.00	800.00
1875S	9	260.00	275.00	325.00	650.00
1876	1	315.00	400.00	500.00	800.00
1876CC	7	280.00	350.00	425.00	650.00
1876S	4	280.00	350.00	425.00	650.00
1877	1	315.00	375.00	450.00	750.00
1877CC	9	280.00	350.00	425.00	650.00
1877S	27	150.00	150.00	175.00	225.00
1878	132	125.00	150.00	175.00	195.00

HALF EAGLES

Date	Thousands Minted	Average Dealers Pay	Average Retail Prices		
			Fine	V. Fine	Ex. Fine
1878CC	9	$500.00	$800.00	$1,000	$2,100
1878S	145	125.00	150.00	175.00	200.00
1879	302	125.00	150.00	175.00	200.00
1879CC	17	210.00	275.00	325.00	400.00
1879S	426	125.00	150.00	175.00	200.00
1880	3,166	125.00	150.00	175.00	200.00
1880CC	51	175.00	275.00	325.00	450.00
1880S	1,349	125.00	150.00	175.00	200.00
1881	5,709	125.00	150.00	175.00	200.00
1881CC	14	210.00	275.00	325.00	400.00
1881S	969	125.00	150.00	175.00	200.00
1882	2,515	125.00	150.00	175.00	200.00
1882CC	83	160.00	200.00	250.00	300.00
1882S	970	125.00	150.00	175.00	200.00
1883	233	125.00	150.00	175.00	200.00
1883CC	13	210.00	275.00	325.00	400.00
1883S	83	125.00	150.00	175.00	200.00
1884	191	125.00	150.00	175.00	200.00
1884CC	16	210.00	275.00	325.00	400.00
1884S	177	125.00	150.00	175.00	200.00
1885	602	125.00	150.00	175.00	200.00
1885S	1,212	125.00	150.00	175.00	200.00
1886	388	125.00	150.00	175.00	200.00
1886S	3,268	125.00	150.00	175.00	200.00
1887	0.09	Rare			
1887S	1,912	125.00	150.00	175.00	200.00
1888	18	125.00	150.00	195.00	225.00
1888S	294	125.00	150.00	175.00	200.00
1889	8	200.00	200.00	225.00	375.00
1890	4	225.00	225.00	250.00	500.00
1890CC	54	160.00	200.00	225.00	300.00
1891	61	125.00	150.00	175.00	200.00
1891CC	208	180.00	200.00	225.00	275.00
1892	754	125.00	150.00	175.00	200.00
1892CC	83	180.00	200.00	225.00	275.00
1892O	10	325.00	400.00	550.00	800.00
1892S	298	125.00	150.00	175.00	200.00
1893	1,528	125.00	150.00	175.00	200.00
1893CC	60	160.00	200.00	225.00	275.00
1893O	110	175.00	225.00	250.00	300.00
1893S	224	125.00	150.00	175.00	200.00
1894	958	125.00	150.00	175.00	200.00
1894O	17	200.00	225.00	250.00	325.00
1894S	56	125.00	150.00	175.00	200.00
1895	1,346	125.00	150.00	175.00	200.00
1895S	112	125.00	150.00	175.00	200.00
1896	59	125.00	150.00	175.00	200.00
1896S	155	125.00	150.00	175.00	200.00
1897	868	125.00	150.00	175.00	200.00

HALF EAGLES

Date	Thousands Minted	Average Dealers Pay	Average Retail Prices		
			Fine	V. Fine	Ex. Fine
1897S	354	$125.00	$150.00	$175.00	$200.00
1898	633	125.00	150.00	175.00	200.00
1898S	1,397	125.00	150.00	175.00	200.00
1899	1,711	125.00	150.00	175.00	200.00
1899S	1,545	125.00	150.00	175.00	200.00
1900	1,406	125.00	150.00	175.00	200.00
1900S	329	125.00	150.00	175.00	200.00
1901	616	125.00	150.00	175.00	200.00
1901S	3,648	125.00	150.00	175.00	200.00
1902	173	125.00	150.00	175.00	200.00
1902S	939	125.00	150.00	175.00	200.00
1903	227	125.00	150.00	175.00	200.00
1903S	1,855	125.00	150.00	175.00	200.00
1904	392	125.00	150.00	175.00	200.00
1904S	97	125.00	150.00	175.00	200.00
1905	302	125.00	150.00	175.00	200.00
1905S	881	125.00	150.00	175.00	200.00
1906	349	125.00	150.00	175.00	200.00
1906D	320	125.00	150.00	175.00	200.00
1906S	598	125.00	150.00	175.00	200.00
1907	626	125.00	150.00	175.00	200.00
1907D	888	125.00	150.00	175.00	200.00
1908	422	125.00	150.00	175.00	200.00

Indian Head Type 1908-1929

FINE—The knot in hair cord must show but small feathers on top of head will be faint.
VERY FINE—Noticeable wear on large middle feathers and tip of eagle's wing.
EX. FINE—Slight wear on cheekbone and jawbone beneath. Top feathers on wing outlined but worn.

1908	578	170.00	200.00	225.00	250.00
1908D	148	170.00	200.00	225.00	250.00
1908S	82	180.00	225.00	250.00	350.00
1909	627	170.00	200.00	225.00	250.00
1909D	3,424	170.00	200.00	225.00	250.00
1909O	34	260.00	450.00	800.00	1,500
1909S	297	170.00	225.00	250.00	350.00
1910	604	170.00	200.00	225.00	250.00
1910D	194	170.00	200.00	225.00	250.00

HALF EAGLES

Date	Thousands Minted	Average Dealers Pay	Average Retail Prices		
			Fine	V. Fine	Ex. Fine
1910S	770	$170.00	$225.00	$250.00	$350.00
1911	915	170.00	200.00	225.00	250.00
1911D	73	190.00	275.00	400.00	625.00
1911S	1,416	170.00	225.00	250.00	350.00
1912	790	170.00	200.00	225.00	250.00
1912S	392	170.00	225.00	250.00	350.00
1913	916	170.00	200.00	225.00	250.00
1913S	408	170.00	225.00	275.00	450.00
1914	247	170.00	200.00	225.00	250.00
1914D	247	170.00	200.00	225.00	250.00
1914S	263	170.00	225.00	250.00	350.00
1915	588	170.00	200.00	225.00	250.00
1915S	164	170.00	250.00	275.00	400.00
1916S	240	170.00	225.00	250.00	350.00
1929	662	1,300	1,750	2,500	4,000

EAGLES ($10.00 Gold Pieces) 1795-1933

Bust Right, Small Eagle 1795-1797

FINE—*Details on turban and head obliterated.*
VERY FINE—*Neck hairlines and details under turban and over forehead are worn, but distinguishable.*
EX. FINE—*Noticeable wear points are: hair left of eye, strand which sweeps across turban and eagle's wing tips.*

1795	6	2,400	3,750	5,500	10,000
1796	4	2,400	3,750	5,500	10,000
1797 Small eagle	4	2,650	4,000	5,750	11,000

EAGLES
Bust Right, Large Eagle 1797-1804

Date	Thousands Minted	Average Dealers Pay	Average Retail Prices		
			Fine	V. Fine	Ex. Fine
1797 Large eagle......	16	$1,050	$1,600	$3,000	$4,500
1798.................	1	2,000	3,750	7,000	11,500
1799.................	32	900.00	1,500	2,000	3,250
1800.................	7	1,100	1,750	2,500	3,750
1801.................	44	900.00	1,500	2,000	3,250
1803.................	15	1,100	1,700	2,300	3,500
1804.................	4	1,300	2,000	3,200	5,500

Coronet Type 1838-1907
No motto over eagle 1838-1866

FINE—*LIBERTY readable but may be slightly worn.*
VERY FINE—*Hairlines above coronet partly worn. Curls under ear worn but defined.*
EX. FINE—*Wear shows at top of head, hair below L in LIBERTY, top of coronet, upper part of wings and neck of eagle.*

1838.................	7	450.00	700.00	1,100	2,000
1839.................	38	350.00	450.00	750.00	1,450

EAGLES

Date	Thousands Minted	Average Dealers Pay	Average Retail Prices		
			Fine	V. Fine	Ex. Fine
1840	47	$240.00	$300.00	$350.00	$450.00
1841	63	240.00	300.00	350.00	450.00
1841O	2	300.00	450.00	600.00	1,250
1842	82	240.00	300.00	350.00	450.00
1842O	27	240.00	300.00	350.00	450.00
1843	75	240.00	300.00	350.00	450.00
1843O	175	240.00	275.00	325.00	425.00
1844	6	285.00	400.00	500.00	900.00
1844O	119	240.00	275.00	325.00	425.00
1845	26	240.00	300.00	350.00	450.00
1845O	47	240.00	275.00	325.00	425.00
1846	20	240.00	300.00	350.00	450.00
1846O	82	240.00	275.00	325.00	425.00
1847	862	240.00	250.00	300.00	375.00
1847O	571	240.00	250.00	300.00	375.00
1848	145	240.00	250.00	300.00	375.00
1848O	36	240.00	275.00	325.00	425.00
1849	654	240.00	250.00	300.00	375.00
1849O	24	240.00	275.00	325.00	425.00
1850	291	240.00	250.00	300.00	375.00
1850O	57	240.00	275.00	325.00	425.00
1851	176	240.00	250.00	300.00	375.00
1851O	263	240.00	250.00	300.00	375.00
1852	263	240.00	250.00	300.00	375.00
1852O	18	240.00	325.00	375.00	475.00
1853	201	240.00	250.00	300.00	375.00
1853O	51	240.00	275.00	325.00	425.00
1854	54	240.00	275.00	325.00	425.00
1854O	52	240.00	275.00	325.00	425.00
1854S	124	240.00	275.00	325.00	425.00
1855	122	240.00	250.00	300.00	375.00
1855O	18	240.00	325.00	375.00	475.00
1855S	9	240.00	500.00	650.00	1,000
1856	60	240.00	250.00	300.00	375.00
1856O	14	240.00	325.00	375.00	475.00
1856S	68	240.00	250.00	300.00	375.00
1857	17	240.00	300.00	350.00	450.00
1857O	5	550.00	650.00	800.00	1,350
1857S	26	240.00	250.00	300.00	375.00
1858	3	2,500	3,000	4,250	6,750
1858O	20	240.00	275.00	325.00	425.00
1858S	12	240.00	325.00	375.00	475.00
1859	16	240.00	275.00	325.00	425.00
1859O	2	500.00	1,000	1,250	2,500
1859S	7	315.00	600.00	750.00	1,250
1860	15	240.00	275.00	325.00	425.00
1860O	11	240.00	325.00	375.00	475.00
1860S	5	350.00	600.00	750.00	1,250
1861	113	240.00	250.00	300.00	375.00

EAGLES

Date	Thousands Minted	Average Dealers Pay	Average Retail Prices		
			Fine	V. Fine	Ex. Fine
1861S	15	$240.00	$275.00	$325.00	$425.00
1862	11	240.00	275.00	325.00	425.00
1862S	12	240.00	275.00	325.00	425.00
1863	1	1,300	1,750	2,500	4,500
1863S	10	285.00	375.00	425.00	850.00
1864	4	400.00	700.00	850.00	1,350
1864S	2	850.00	1,100	1,800	3,250
1865	4	325.00	625.00	775.00	1,150
1865S	17	300.00	625.00	775.00	1,150
1866S	8	450.00	750.00	1,000	1,700

Motto over eagle 1866-1907

FINE—*All letters in LIBERTY are complete.*
VERY FINE—*Half of hairlines over coronet visible. Curls under ear worn but defined. IN GOD WE TRUST and its ribbon are sharp.*
EX. FINE—*Wear shows at top of head, hair below L in LIBERTY, top of coronet, upper part of wings and neck of eagle.*

1866	4	315.00	400.00	450.00	550.00
1866S	12	300.00	350.00	400.00	500.00
1867	3	300.00	400.00	450.00	550.00
1867S	9	275.00	350.00	400.00	525.00
1868	11	275.00	350.00	400.00	500.00
1868S	13	275.00	350.00	400.00	500.00
1869	2	450.00	500.00	650.00	1,100
1869S	6	275.00	350.00	400.00	525.00
1870	4	300.00	400.00	450.00	550.00
1870CC	6	650.00	700.00	950.00	2,500
1870S	8	275.00	350.00	400.00	525.00
1871	2	450.00	500.00	650.00	1,100
1871CC	8	450.00	500.00	650.00	1,100
1871S	16	275.00	325.00	375.00	475.00
1872	2	500.00	750.00	875.00	1,450
1872CC	5	400.00	450.00	525.00	900.00
1872S	17	275.00	325.00	375.00	475.00
1873	0.8	950.00	1,000	1,250	2,500
1873CC	5	625.00	725.00	975.00	1,500

EAGLES

Date	Thousands Minted	Average Dealers Pay	Average Retail Prices Fine	V. Fine	Ex. Fine
1873S	12	$275.00	$325.00	$375.00	$475.00
1874	53	240.00	250.00	300.00	325.00
1874CC	17	240.00	325.00	375.00	475.00
1874S	10	280.00	300.00	350.00	450.00
1875	0.1	Rare			
1875CC	8	400.00	425.00	500.00	750.00
1876	0.7	750.00	900.00	1,100	2,500
1876CC	5	475.00	600.00	700.00	1,100
1876S	5	315.00	400.00	450.00	650.00
1877	0.8	950.00	1,100	1,400	2,750
1877CC	3	550.00	800.00	900.00	1,500
1877S	17	225.00	275.00	325.00	400.00
1878	74	200.00	225.00	275.00	300.00
1878CC	3	575.00	800.00	900.00	1,500
1878S	26	225.00	225.00	275.00	300.00
1879	385	200.00	225.00	275.00	300.00
1879CC	2	1,250	1,750	2,250	4,250
1879O	1	600.00	750.00	1,000	1,750
1879S	224	200.00	225.00	275.00	300.00
1880	1,645	200.00	225.00	275.00	300.00
1880CC	11	240.00	275.00	325.00	450.00
1880O	9	280.00	275.00	325.00	450.00
1880S	506	200.00	225.00	275.00	300.00
1881	3,877	200.00	225.00	275.00	300.00
1881CC	24	240.00	275.00	325.00	450.00
1881O	8	280.00	300.00	350.00	475.00
1881S	970	200.00	225.00	275.00	300.00
1882	2,324	200.00	225.00	275.00	300.00
1882CC	7	280.00	300.00	350.00	475.00
1882O	11	250.00	275.00	325.00	425.00
1882S	132	200.00	225.00	275.00	300.00
1883	209	200.00	225.00	275.00	300.00
1883CC	12	280.00	300.00	350.00	475.00
1883O	0.8	1,000	1,300	1,850	3,000
1883S	38	200.00	225.00	275.00	300.00
1884	77	200.00	225.00	275.00	300.00
1884CC	10	280.00	300.00	350.00	500.00
1884S	124	200.00	225.00	275.00	300.00
1885	254	200.00	225.00	275.00	300.00
1885S	228	200.00	225.00	275.00	300.00
1886	236	200.00	225.00	275.00	300.00
1886S	826	200.00	225.00	275.00	300.00
1887	54	200.00	225.00	275.00	300.00
1887S	817	200.00	225.00	275.00	300.00
1888	133	200.00	225.00	275.00	300.00
1888O	21	200.00	250.00	300.00	325.00
1888S	649	200.00	225.00	275.00	300.00
1889	4	300.00	350.00	400.00	575.00
1889S	425	200.00	225.00	275.00	300.00

EAGLES

Date	Thousands Minted	Average Dealers Pay	Average Retail Prices		
			Fine	V. Fine	Ex. Fine
1890	58	$240.00	$250.00	$300.00	$325.00
1890CC	17	200.00	250.00	300.00	325.00
1891	92	200.00	225.00	275.00	300.00
1891CC	104	200.00	250.00	300.00	325.00
1892	798	200.00	225.00	275.00	300.00
1892CC	40	250.00	275.00	325.00	425.00
1892O	29	200.00	250.00	300.00	325.00
1892S	115	200.00	225.00	275.00	300.00
1893	1,841	200.00	225.00	275.00	300.00
1893CC	14	240.00	300.00	350.00	475.00
1893O	17	240.00	275.00	325.00	425.00
1893S	141	200.00	225.00	275.00	300.00
1894	2,471	200.00	225.00	275.00	300.00
1894O	107	200.00	225.00	275.00	300.00
1894S	25	200.00	225.00	275.00	300.00
1895	568	200.00	225.00	275.00	300.00
1895O	98	200.00	225.00	275.00	300.00
1895S	49	200.00	225.00	275.00	300.00
1896	76	200.00	225.00	275.00	300.00
1896S	124	200.00	225.00	275.00	300.00
1897	1,000	200.00	225.00	275.00	300.00
1897O	42	200.00	225.00	275.00	300.00
1897S	235	200.00	225.00	275.00	300.00
1898	812	200.00	225.00	275.00	300.00
1898S	474	200.00	225.00	275.00	300.00
1899	1,262	200.00	225.00	275.00	300.00
1899O	37	200.00	225.00	275.00	300.00
1899S	841	200.00	225.00	275.00	300.00
1900	294	200.00	225.00	275.00	300.00
1900S	81	200.00	225.00	275.00	300.00
1901	1,719	200.00	225.00	275.00	300.00
1901O	72	200.00	225.00	275.00	300.00
1901S	2,813	200.00	225.00	275.00	300.00
1902	83	200.00	225.00	275.00	300.00
1902S	469	200.00	225.00	275.00	300.00
1903	126	200.00	225.00	275.00	300.00
1903O	113	200.00	225.00	275.00	300.00
1903S	538	200.00	225.00	275.00	300.00
1904	162	200.00	225.00	275.00	300.00
1904O	109	200.00	225.00	275.00	300.00
1905	201	200.00	225.00	275.00	300.00
1905S	369	200.00	225.00	275.00	300.00
1906	165	200.00	225.00	275.00	300.00
1906D	981	200.00	225.00	275.00	300.00
1906O	87	200.00	225.00	275.00	300.00
1906S	457	200.00	225.00	275.00	300.00
1907	1,204	200.00	225.00	275.00	300.00
1907D	1,030	200.00	225.00	275.00	300.00
1907S	210	200.00	225.00	275.00	300.00

EAGLES
Indian Head Type 1907-1933

FINE—*Feathers on bonnet show definite wear. Full LIBERTY.*
VERY FINE—*Bonnet feathers worn near band. Hair high points show wear.*
EX. FINE—*Trace of wear on cheekbone, feathers on headdress, above eagle's eye and left wing.*

Date	Thousands Minted	Average Dealers Pay	Average Retail Prices		
			Fine	V. Fine	Ex. Fine
1907	239	$285.00	$350.00	$425.00	$500.00
1908	33	285.00	350.00	425.00	500.00
1908D	210	280.00	350.00	425.00	475.00

Motto "In God We Trust" added

1908	341	275.00	350.00	425.00	450.00
1908D	836	275.00	350.00	425.00	450.00
1908S	60	280.00	350.00	425.00	450.00
1909	185	275.00	350.00	425.00	450.00
1909D	122	275.00	350.00	425.00	450.00
1909S	292	280.00	350.00	425.00	450.00
1910	319	275.00	350.00	425.00	450.00
1910D	2,357	275.00	350.00	425.00	450.00
1910S	811	275.00	350.00	425.00	450.00
1911	506	275.00	350.00	425.00	450.00
1911D	30	300.00	375.00	450.00	750.00
1911S	51	280.00	350.00	425.00	450.00
1912	405	275.00	350.00	425.00	450.00
1912S	300	275.00	350.00	425.00	450.00
1913	442	275.00	350.00	425.00	450.00
1913S	66	300.00	375.00	450.00	650.00
1914	151	275.00	350.00	425.00	450.00
1914D	344	275.00	350.00	425.00	450.00
1914S	208	275.00	350.00	425.00	450.00
1915	351	275.00	350.00	425.00	450.00
1915S	59	275.00	350.00	425.00	450.00
1916S	139	275.00	350.00	425.00	450.00
1920S	127	3,000	3,000	4,500	7,500
1926	1,014	275.00	350.00	425.00	450.00
1930S	96	1,250	2,000	3,000	4,000
1932	4,463	275.00	350.00	425.00	450.00
1933	312	Rare			

DOUBLE EAGLES ($20.00 Gold Pieces) 1849-1933
Liberty Head Type 1849-1907

FINE—*LIBERTY worn but readable. All hairlines show considerable wear.*
VERY FINE—*LIBERTY is bold. Jewels on crown defined. Lower half worn flat. Hair worn about ear.*
EX. FINE—*Slight wear on curls and crown jewels. Tiny bagmarks.*

Date	Thousands Minted	Average Dealers Pay	Average Retail Prices		
			Fine	V. Fine	Ex. Fine
1849	....	Rare			
1850	1,170	$425.00	$475.00	$550.00	$675.00
1850O	141	475.00	550.00	625.00	800.00
1851	2,087	425.00	475.00	550.00	675.00
1851O	315	475.00	550.00	625.00	800.00
1852	2,053	425.00	475.00	550.00	675.00
1852O	190	475.00	550.00	625.00	800.00
1853	1,261	425.00	475.00	550.00	675.00
1853O	71	475.00	550.00	625.00	800.00
1854	758	425.00	475.00	550.00	675.00
1854O	3	Rare			45,000
1854S	141	425.00	475.00	550.00	675.00
1855	365	425.00	475.00	550.00	675.00
1855O	8	800.00	900.00	1,200	2,000
1855S	880	425.00	475.00	550.00	675.00
1856	330	425.00	475.00	550.00	675.00
1856O	2	Rare			35,000
1856S	1,190	425.00	475.00	550.00	675.00
1857	439	425.00	475.00	550.00	675.00
1857O	30	475.00	550.00	625.00	800.00
1857S	971	425.00	475.00	550.00	675.00
1858	212	425.00	475.00	550.00	675.00
1858O	35	475.00	550.00	625.00	800.00
1858S	847	425.00	475.00	550.00	675.00

DOUBLE EAGLES

Date	Thousands Minted	Average Dealers Pay	Average Retail Prices		
			Fine	V. Fine	Ex. Fine
1859	44	$425.00	$475.00	$550.00	$675.00
1859O	9	900.00	1,100	1,500	2,500
1859S	636	425.00	475.00	550.00	675.00
1860	578	425.00	475.00	550.00	675.00
1860O	7	1,350	1,400	2,000	3,250
1860S	545	425.00	475.00	550.00	675.00
1861	2,976	425.00	475.00	550.00	675.00
1861O	18	800.00	800.00	1,100	2,000
1861S	768	425.00	475.00	550.00	675.00
1862	92	425.00	475.00	550.00	675.00
1862S	854	425.00	475.00	500.00	675.00
1863	143	425.00	475.00	550.00	675.00
1863S	967	425.00	475.00	550.00	675.00
1864	204	425.00	475.00	550.00	675.00
1864S	794	425.00	475.00	550.00	675.00
1865	351	425.00	475.00	550.00	675.00
1865S	1,043	425.00	475.00	550.00	675.00
1866S No motto		450.00	475.00	550.00	675.00

1866 Motto	699	400.00	450.00	525.00	550.00
1866S Motto	842	400.00	450.00	525.00	550.00
1867	251	400.00	450.00	525.00	550.00
1867S	921	400.00	450.00	525.00	550.00
1868	99	400.00	450.00	525.00	550.00
1868S	838	400.00	450.00	525.00	550.00
1869	175	400.00	450.00	525.00	550.00
1869S	687	400.00	450.00	525.00	550.00
1870	155	400.00	450.00	525.00	550.00
1870CC	4	Rare		13,000	25,000
1870S	982	400.00	450.00	525.00	550.00
1871	80	400.00	450.00	525.00	550.00
1871CC	17	750.00	1,000	1,400	2,250
1871S	928	400.00	450.00	525.00	550.00

DOUBLE EAGLES

Date	Thousands Minted	Average Dealers Pay	Average Retail Prices		
			Fine	V. Fine	Ex. Fine
1872	252	$400.00	$450.00	$525.00	$550.00
1872CC	27	700.00	600.00	675.00	900.00
1872S	780	400.00	450.00	525.00	550.00
1873	1,710	400.00	450.00	525.00	550.00
1873CC	22	650.00	575.00	650.00	750.00
1873S	1,041	400.00	450.00	525.00	550.00
1874	367	400.00	450.00	525.00	550.00
1874CC	115	450.00	500.00	575.00	700.00
1874S	1,214	400.00	450.00	525.00	550.00
1875	296	400.00	450.00	525.00	550.00
1875CC	111	450.00	500.00	575.00	700.00
1875S	1,230	400.00	450.00	525.00	550.00
1876	584	400.00	450.00	525.00	550.00
1876CC	138	450.00	500.00	575.00	700.00
1876S	1,597	400.00	450.00	525.00	550.00
1877	398	400.00	450.00	500.00	525.00
1877CC	43	450.00	600.00	700.00	800.00
1877S	1,735	400.00	450.00	500.00	525.00
1878	544	400.00	450.00	500.00	525.00
1878CC	13	550.00	650.00	750.00	850.00
1878S	1,739	400.00	450.00	500.00	525.00
1879	208	400.00	450.00	500.00	525.00
1879CC	11	650.00	700.00	800.00	1,350
1879O	2	2,000	2,000	2,500	3,750
1879S	1,224	400.00	450.00	500.00	525.00
1880	51	400.00	450.00	500.00	550.00
1880S	836	400.00	450.00	500.00	525.00
1881	2	1,600	1,850	2,250	4,250
1881S	727	400.00	450.00	500.00	525.00
1882	0.6	2,400	2,500	3,500	9,000
1882CC	39	450.00	575.00	650.00	800.00
1882S	1,125	400.00	450.00	500.00	525.00
1883	0.09	Rare			
1883CC	60	450.00	575.00	650.00	750.00
1883S	1,189	400.00	450.00	500.00	525.00
1884	0.07	Rare			
1884CC	81	450.00	575.00	650.00	750.00
1884S	916	400.00	450.00	500.00	525.00
1885	0.8	2,300	2,500	3,250	8,000
1885CC	9	650.00	700.00	800.00	1,100
1885S	684	400.00	450.00	500.00	525.00
1886	1	2,300	2,750	3,500	8,500
1887	0.1	Rare			
1887S	283	400.00	450.00	500.00	525.00
1888	226	400.00	450.00	500.00	525.00
1888S	860	400.00	450.00	500.00	525.00
1889	44	400.00	450.00	500.00	525.00
1889CC	31	450.00	475.00	550.00	650.00
1889S	775	400.00	450.00	500.00	525.00

DOUBLE EAGLES

Date	Thousands Minted	Average Dealers Pay	Average Retail Prices		
			Fine	V. Fine	Ex. Fine
1890	76	$400.00	$450.00	$500.00	$525.00
1890CC	91	600.00	500.00	550.00	650.00
1890S	803	400.00	450.00	500.00	525.00
1891	1	750.00	800.00	1,250	2,750
1891CC	5	700.00	750.00	1,200	2,000
1891S	1,288	400.00	450.00	500.00	525.00
1892	5	650.00	750.00	1,000	1,850
1892CC	27	500.00	550.00	650.00	800.00
1892S	930	400.00	450.00	500.00	525.00
1893	344	400.00	450.00	500.00	525.00
1893CC	18	525.00	600.00	675.00	825.00
1893S	996	400.00	450.00	500.00	525.00
1894	1,369	400.00	450.00	500.00	525.00
1894S	1,049	400.00	450.00	500.00	525.00
1895	1,115	400.00	450.00	500.00	525.00
1895S	1,144	400.00	450.00	500.00	525.00
1896	793	400.00	450.00	500.00	525.00
1896S	1,404	400.00	450.00	500.00	525.00
1897	1,383	400.00	450.00	500.00	525.00
1897S	1,470	400.00	450.00	500.00	525.00
1898	170	400.00	450.00	500.00	525.00
1898S	2,575	400.00	450.00	500.00	525.00
1899	1,669	400.00	450.00	500.00	525.00
1899S	2,010	400.00	450.00	500.00	525.00
1900	1,875	400.00	450.00	500.00	525.00
1900S	2,460	400.00	450.00	500.00	525.00
1901	112	400.00	450.00	500.00	525.00
1901S	1,596	400.00	450.00	500.00	525.00
1902	31	400.00	450.00	500.00	525.00
1902S	1,754	400.00	450.00	500.00	525.00
1903	287	400.00	450.00	500.00	525.00
1903S	954	400.00	450.00	500.00	525.00
1904	6,257	400.00	450.00	500.00	525.00
1904S	5,134	400.00	450.00	500.00	525.00
1905	59	400.00	450.00	500.00	525.00
1905S	1,813	400.00	450.00	500.00	525.00
1906	70	400.00	450.00	500.00	525.00
1906D	620	400.00	450.00	500.00	525.00
1906S	2,066	400.00	450.00	500.00	525.00
1907	1,452	400.00	450.00	500.00	525.00
1907D	842	400.00	450.00	500.00	525.00
1907S	2,166	400.00	450.00	500.00	525.00

Values shown in these listings are averages of prices quoted by dealers throughout the country. The publisher of this book does not buy, sell, or appraise coins.

DOUBLE EAGLES

Saint-Gaudens Type 1907-1932

Augustus Saint-Gaudens designed this $20.00 gold piece, our country's most beautiful coin. His monogram is below the date. Mint marks, when used, are located above the date. A special variety minted in 1907 has the date in Roman numerals and the design in very high relief. Coins dated 1933 were minted but were not placed in circulation.

FINE—Wear evident on full length of right leg. Drapery at chest worn flat. Leaves beneath date worn. Eagle's wing tips worn noticeably.
VERY FINE—Minor wear on legs and toes. Eagle's left wing and breast feathers worn.
EXTRA FINE—Drapery lines on chest visible. Wear on right breast, knee and below. Eagle's feathers on breast and right wing are bold.

Date	Thousands Minted	Average Dealers Pay	Average Retail Prices		
			Fine	V. Fine	Ex. Fine
1907 MCMVII	11	$1,000	$1,500	$3,250	$5,000
1907	362	450.00	500.00	575.00	650.00
1908	4,272	450.00	500.00	575.00	625.00
1908D	664	450.00	500.00	575.00	625.00

DOUBLE EAGLES
Motto "In God We Trust" added

Date	Thousands Minted	Average Dealers Pay	Average Retail Prices		
			Fine	V. Fine	Ex. Fine
1908	156	$450.00	$500.00	$575.00	$600.00
1908D	350	450.00	500.00	575.00	600.00
1908S	22	500.00	675.00	800.00	1,500
1909	161	450.00	500.00	575.00	600.00
1909D	53	500.00	650.00	800.00	1,000
1909S	2,775	450.00	500.00	575.00	600.00
1910	482	450.00	500.00	575.00	600.00
1910D	429	450.00	500.00	575.00	600.00
1910S	2,128	450.00	500.00	575.00	600.00
1911	197	450.00	500.00	575.00	600.00
1911D	847	450.00	500.00	575.00	600.00
1911S	776	450.00	500.00	575.00	600.00
1912	150	450.00	600.00	700.00	800.00
1913	169	450.00	500.00	575.00	600.00
1913D	394	450.00	500.00	575.00	600.00
1913S	34	450.00	550.00	600.00	700.00
1914	95	450.00	500.00	575.00	600.00
1914D	453	450.00	500.00	575.00	600.00
1914S	1,498	450.00	500.00	575.00	600.00
1915	152	450.00	500.00	575.00	600.00
1915S	568	450.00	500.00	575.00	600.00
1916S	796	450.00	600.00	700.00	800.00
1920	228	450.00	500.00	575.00	600.00
1920S	558	2,200	4,000	6,500	10,000
1921	529	2,700	5,000	9,000	14,000
1922	1,376	450.00	500.00	575.00	600.00
1922S	2,658	450.00	600.00	700.00	850.00
1923	566	450.00	500.00	575.00	600.00
1923D	1,702	450.00	500.00	575.00	600.00
1924	4,324	450.00	500.00	575.00	600.00
1924D	3,050	500.00	650.00	850.00	1,000
1924S	2,928	500.00	650.00	850.00	1,000
1925	2,832	500.00	500.00	575.00	600.00
1925D	2,939	500.00	675.00	900.00	1,200
1925S	3,777	500.00	650.00	775.00	900.00
1926	817	450.00	500.00	575.00	600.00
1926D	481	500.00	675.00	950.00	1,300
1926S	2,042	500.00	650.00	775.00	900.00
1927	2,947	450.00	500.00	575.00	600.00
1927D	180	Rare			
1927S	3,107	1,200			5,750
1928	8,816	450.00	500.00	575.00	600.00
1929	1,780	1,500			6,000
1930S	74	3,500			15,000
1931	2,938	2,000			9,000
1931D	107	2,500			10,000
1932	1,102	2,200			11,000

COMMEMORATIVE SILVER COINS

In 1892, to commemorate the World's Columbian Exposition in Chicago, Congress authorized the coinage of a special half dollar and quarter dollar, thus starting a long line of United States commemorative coins. All commemorative coins have been distributed by private individuals or commissions; they paid the mint the face value of the coins and in turn sold the pieces at a premium to collectors.

The commemorative coin series is collected generally in uncirculated condition and the common varieties that have been circulated are practically unsalable. Even the rare varieties are sold at great discount when in anything but mint state.

Due to their different designs and the events they commemorate this is a popular series and is worthy of the consideration of every American collector.

Commemorative totals are given as "quantity available." In many instances a portion of the total coinage has been melted. The figures given here represent the quantity of coins that are still in the hands of collectors and dealers.

		Quantity Available	Buy Unc.	Sell Unc.
1893	Isabella Quarter	24,214	$400.00	$500.00

| 1900 | Lafayette Dollar | 36,026 | 1,200 | 1,500 |

COMMEMORATIVE SILVER HALF DOLLARS

(Listed alphabetically)

2x2 in Field

		Quantity Available	Buy Unc.	Sell Unc.
1921	Alabama, "2 x 2" in field........	6,006	$385.00	$475.00
1921	Same, no "2 x 2"	59,038	315.00	390.00

1936	Albany, New York.............	17,671	250.00	325.00

1937	Battle of Antietam 1862-1937....	18,028	350.00	420.00

COMMEMORATIVE SILVER

		Quantity Available		Buy Unc.	Sell Unc.
1935	Arkansas Centennial	13,012			
1935D	Same	5,505	Set	$225.00	$275.00
1935S	Same	5,506			
1936	Arkansas Centennial	9,660			
1936D	Same	9,660	Set	225.00	275.00
1936S	Same	9,662			
1937	Arkansas Centennial	5,505			
1937D	Same	5,505	Set	235.00	300.00
1937S	Same	5,506			
1938	Arkansas Centennial	3,156			
1938D	Same	3,155	Set	425.00	525.00
1938S	Same	3,156			
1939	Arkansas Centennial	2,104			
1939D	Same	2,104	Set	1,200	1,500
1939S	Same	2,105			
	Single type coin			60.00	70.00

1936S	Bay Bridge, S.F.-Oakland	71,424	85.00	100.00

COMMEMORATIVE SILVER

		Quantity Available	Buy Unc.	Sell Unc.
1934	Daniel Boone Bicentennial	10,007	$100.00	$120.00
1935	Boone Bicentennial	10,010 ⎫		
1935D	Same	5,005 ⎬ Set	240.00	325.00
1935S	Same	5,005 ⎭		

1935	Boone (small 1934 added)	⎫		
1935D	Same	2,003 ⎬ Set	1,200	1,600
1935S	Same	2,004 ⎭		
1936	Boone Bicentennial	12,012 ⎫		
1936D	Same	5,005 ⎬ Set	240.00	325.00
1936S	Same	5,006 ⎭		
1937	Boone Bicentennial	9,810 ⎫		
1937D	Same	2,506 ⎬ Set	550.00	700.00
1937S	Same	2,506 ⎭		
1938	Boone Bicentennial	2,100 ⎫		
1938D	Same	2,100 ⎬ Set	1,100	1,450
1938S	Same	2,100 ⎭		
	Single type coin		85.00	110.00

COMMEMORATIVE SILVER

		Quantity Available	Buy Unc.	Sell Unc.
1936	Bridgeport, Conn., Centennial	25,015	$125.00	$165.00

| 1925S | California Diamond Jubilee | 86,594 | 135.00 | 175.00 |

1936	Cincinnati Musical Center	5,005		
1936D	Same	5,005	Set 1,000	1,400
1936S	Same	5,006		
	Single type coin		315.00	400.00

[145]

COMMEMORATIVE SILVER

 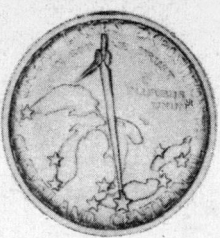

		Quantity Available	Buy Unc.	Sell Unc.
1936	Cleveland, Great Lakes Expo	50,030	$70.00	$85.00

1936	Columbia, S.C., Sesqui	9,007		
1936D	Same	8,009 } Set	825.00	1,000
1936S	Same	8,007		
	Single type coin		250.00	325.00

1892	Columbian Exposition	950,000	18.00	25.00
1893	Same	1,550,405	17.00	22.00

COMMEMORATIVE SILVER

		Quantity Available	Buy Unc.	Sell Unc.
1935	Connecticut Tercentenary	25,018	$190.00	$250.00

		Quantity Available	Buy Unc.	Sell Unc.
1936	Delaware Tercentenary	20,993	200.00	250.00

		Quantity Available	Buy Unc.	Sell Unc.
1936	Elgin, Illinois, Centennial	20,015	180.00	225.00

COMMEMORATIVE SILVER

		Quantity Available	Buy Unc.	Sell Unc.
1936	Battle of Gettysburg	26,928	$275.00	$325.00

| 1922 | Grant Memorial, star in obv. field. | 4,256 | 650.00 | 800.00 |
| 1922 | Same, no star in obv. field | 67,405 | 80.00 | 100.00 |

| 1928 | Hawaiian Sesquicentennial | 10,008 | 1,250 | 1,500 |

COMMEMORATIVE SILVER

		Quantity Available	Buy Unc.	Sell Unc.
1935	Hudson, N.Y. Sesquicentennial	10,008	$650.00	$800.00

| 1924 | Huguenot-Walloon Tercentenary | 142,080 | 80.00 | 100.00 |

| 1946 | Iowa Centennial | 100,057 | 70.00 | 90.00 |

COMMEMORATIVE SILVER

		Quantity Available	Buy Unc.	Sell Unc.
1925	Lexington-Concord Sesquicentennial	162,013	$57.50	$80.00

| 1918 | Lincoln-Illinois Centennial | 100,058 | 75.00 | 90.00 |

| 1936 | Long Island Tercentenary | 81,826 | 55.00 | 75.00 |

COMMEMORATIVE SILVER

		Quantity Available	Buy Unc.	Sell Unc.
1936	Lynchburg, Va., Sesquicentennial	20,013	$175.00	$215.00

| 1920 | Maine Centennial .... | 50,028 | 95.00 | 120.00 |

| 1934 | Maryland Tercentenary .... | 25,015 | 150.00 | 190.00 |

COMMEMORATIVE SILVER

2 ★ 4 in field

		Quantity Available	Buy Unc.	Sell Unc.
1921	Missouri Centennial, "2 ★ 4"	5,000	$750.00	$900.00
1921	Same, No "2 ★ 4"	15,428	725.00	875.00

1923S	Monroe Doctrine Centennial	274,077	45.00	60.00

1938	New Rochelle, N.Y. 1688-1938	15,266	300.00	400.00

COMMEMORATIVE SILVER

		Quantity Available	Buy Unc.	Sell Unc.
1936	Norfolk, Va., Bicentennial..	16,936	$325.00	$400.00

1926	Oregon Trail Memorial	47,955	100.00	130.00
1926S	Same...........................	83,055	100.00	130.00
1928	Oregon Trail Memorial	6,028	220.00	280.00
1933D	Oregon Trail Memorial	5,008	250.00	325.00
1934D	Oregon Trail Memorial	7,006	175.00	235.00
1936	Oregon Trail Memorial	10,006	110.00	150.00
1936S	Same...........................	5,006	170.00	225.00
1937D	Oregon Trail Memorial	12,008	100.00	150.00
1938	Oregon Trail Memorial ...... 6,006 ⎫			
1938D	Same........................ 6,005 ⎬ Set		475.00	575.00
1938S	Same........................ 6,006 ⎭			
1939	Oregon Trail Memorial ...... 3,004 ⎫			
1939D	Same........................ 3,004 ⎬ Set		750.00	925.00
1939S	Same........................ 3,005 ⎭			
	Single type coin		100.00	130.00

COMMEMORATIVE SILVER

		Quantity Available	Buy Unc.	Sell Unc.
1915S	Panama Pacific Exposition	27,134	$675.00	$850.00

1920	Pilgrim Tercentenary	152,112	50.00	70.00
1921	Same	20,053	130.00	200.00

1936	Rhode Island Tercentenary	20,013		
1936D	Same	15,010 } Set	450.00	575.00
1936S	Same	15,011		
	Single type coin		135.00	175.00

COMMEMORATIVE SILVER

		Quantity Available	Buy Unc.	Sell Unc.
1937	Roanoke Island, N.C., 1587-1937	29,030	$130.00	$175.00

| 1936 | Arkansas Centennial (Robinson) | 25,265 | 110.00 | 150.00 |

| 1935S | San Diego, California-Pacific Expo | 70,132 | 55.00 | 75.00 |
| 1936D | Same | 30,092 | 100.00 | 120.00 |

[155]

COMMEMORATIVE SILVER

		Quantity Available	Buy Unc.	Sell Unc.
1926	Sesquicentennial of American Independence	141,120	$45.00	$60.00

| 1935 | Old Spanish Trail 1535-1935 | 10,008 | 800.00 | 1,000 |

| 1925 | Stone Mountain Memorial | 1,314,709 | 23.00 | 33.00 |

COMMEMORATIVE SILVER

		Quantity Available	Buy Unc.	Sell Unc.
1934	Texas Centennial	61,463	$70.00	$100.00
1935	Texas Centennial	9,996 ⎫		
1935D	Same	10,007 ⎬ Set	220.00	280.00
1935S	Same	10,008 ⎭		
1936	Texas Centennial	8,911 ⎫		
1936D	Same	9,039 ⎬ Set	220.00	280.00
1936S	Same	9,055 ⎭		
1937	Texas Centennial	6,571 ⎫		
1937D	Same	6,605 ⎬ Set	265.00	350.00
1937S	Same	6,637 ⎭		
1938	Texas Centennial	3,780 ⎫		
1938D	Same	3,775 ⎬ Set	525.00	625.00
1938S	Same	3,814 ⎭		
	Single type coin		70.00	90.00

1925	Fort Vancouver Centennial	14,994	480.00	570.00

COMMEMORATIVE SILVER

	Quantity Available	Buy Unc.	Sell Unc.
1927 Vermont Sesquicentennial	28,162	$215.00	$275.00

1946	Booker T. Washington ... 1,000,546			
1946D	Same 200,113	Set	35.00	50.00
1946S	Same 500,279			
1947	Booker T. Washington 100,017			
1947D	Same 100,017	Set	47.50	60.00
1947S	Same 100,017			
1948	Booker T. Washington 8,005			
1948D	Same 8,005	Set	80.00	100.00
1948S	Same 8,005			
1949	Booker T. Washington 6,004			
1949D	Same 6,004	Set	150.00	200.00
1949S	Same 6,004			
1950	Booker T. Washington 6,004			
1950D	Same 6,004	Set	110.00	160.00
1950S	Same 512,091			
1951	Booker T. Washington 510,082			
1951D	Same 7,004	Set	95.00	125.00
1951S	Same 7,004			
	Single type coin		10.00	16.00

COMMEMORATIVE SILVER

		Quantity Available		Buy Unc.	Sell Unc.
1951	Washington-Carver	110,018	⎫		
1951D	Same	10,004	⎬ Set	$60.00	$80.00
1951S	Same	10,004	⎭		
1952	Washington-Carver	2,006,292	⎫		
1952D	Same	8,006	⎬ Set	75.00	110.00
1952S	Same	8,006	⎭		
1953	Washington-Carver	8,003	⎫		
1953D	Same	8,003	⎬ Set	125.00	165.00
1953S	Same	108,020	⎭		
1954	Washington-Carver	12,006	⎫		
1954D	Same	12,006	⎬ Set	60.00	80.00
1954S	Same	122,024	⎭		
	Single type coin			10.00	16.00

1936	Wisconsin Centennial	25,015	130.00	190.00

COMMEMORATIVE SILVER

		Quantity Available	Buy Unc.	Sell Unc.
1936	York County, Maine Centennial	25,015	$125.00	$170.00

COMMEMORATIVE GOLD COINS

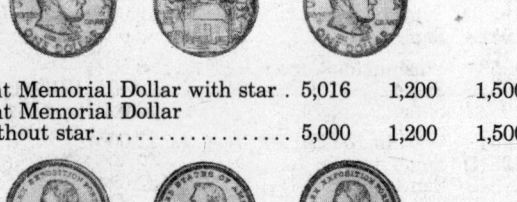

		Quantity	Buy	Sell
1922	Grant Memorial Dollar with star	5,016	1,200	1,500
1922	Grant Memorial Dollar without star	5,000	1,200	1,500

1904	Lewis and Clark Exposition Dollar	10,025	1,700	2,100
1905	Lewis and Clark Exposition Dollar	10,041	1,700	2,100

1903	Louisiana Purchase Jefferson Dollar	17,500	700.00	925.00
1903	Louisiana Purchase McKinley Dollar	17,500	700.00	925.00

COMMEMORATIVE GOLD

		Quantity Available	Buy Unc.	Sell Unc.
1916	McKinley Memorial Dollar	9,977	$700.00	$1,000
1917	McKinley Memorial Dollar	10,000	775.00	1,100

1915S	Panama Pacific Exposition Dollar	15,000	850.00	1,100
1915S	Panama Pacific Exposition $2.50	6,749	1,800	2,400

1915S	Panama Pacific $50 Round	483	21,000	30,000
1915S	Panama Pacific $50 Octagonal	645	16,000	24,000

1926	Philadelphia Sesquicentennial $2.50	46,019	550.00	750.00

PRIVATE OR TERRITORIAL GOLD COINS

The words "Private Gold," used with reference to coins struck outside of the United States Mint, are a general term. In the sense that no state or territory had authority to coin money, private gold simply refers to those interesting necessity pieces of various shapes, denominations and degrees of intrinsic worth which were circulated in isolated areas of our country by individuals, assayers, bankers, etc. Some will use the words "Territorial" and "State" to cover certain issues because they were coined and circulated in a Territory or State. While the state of California properly sanctioned the ingots stamped by F. D. Kohler as state assayer, in no instance were any of the gold pieces struck by authority of any of the territorial governments.

The stamped ingots put out by Augustus Humbert, the United States assayer of gold, were not recognized at the United States Mint as an official issue of coins, but simply as ingots, though Humbert placed the value and fineness on the pieces as an official agent of the federal government.

Private coins were circulated in most instances because of a shortage of regular coinage. In the western states particularly, money became so scarce that the very commodity which the pioneers had come so far to acquire was converted into a local medium of exchange.

Values shown are average retail prices.

TEMPLETON REID
Georgia 1830

1830 $2.50		$25,000
1830 $5.00		RARE
1830 $10.00		RARE

PRIVATE GOLD

THE BECHTLERS

Rutherford County, N. C. 1830-1852

```
$1.00............................................. $400.00
$2.50.............................................  700.00
$5.00.............................................  850.00
```

NORRIS, GRIEG & NORRIS

San Francisco 1849

 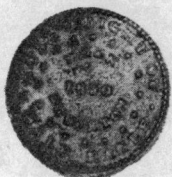

```
1849  $5.00 ....................................... $900.00
1850  $5.00 .........................................  RARE
```

MOFFAT & CO.

San Francisco 1849-1853

```
GOLD INGOTS OF VARIOUS DENOMINATIONS ........ RARE
1849  $5.00 ....................................... $550.00
1850  $5.00 .......................................  550.00
1849  $10.00 .....................................  1,300
```

PRIVATE GOLD

UNITED STATES ASSAY OFFICE OF GOLD

 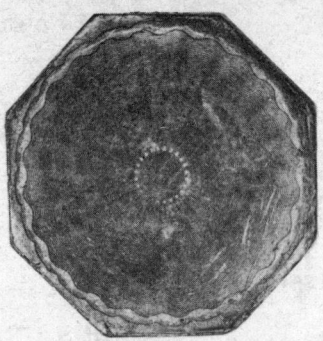

$50.00 .... $4,500

1852 $10.00 MOFFAT AND CO. $950.00
1853 $20.00 MOFFAT AND CO. 1,000

1852 $10.00 .... $800.00
1853 $10.00 1,200
1852 $20.00 3,000
1853 $20.00 ....   750.00

PRIVATE GOLD

CINCINNATI MINING & TRADING CO.

1849 $5.00 .... RARE
1849 $10.00 .... RARE
    (Beware of spurious specimens cast in base metal.)

MASSACHUSETTS AND CALIFORNIA COMPANY
San Francisco 1849

1849 $5.00 .... $20,000

MINERS' BANK
San Francisco 1849

1849 $10.00 .... $6,000

PRIVATE GOLD
J. S. ORMSBY
Sacramento 1849

1849 $5.00 .... RARE
1849 $10.00 .... $35,000

PACIFIC COMPANY
San Francisco 1849

1849 $5.00 .... RARE
1849 $10.00 .... $15,000

F. D. KOHLER
California State Assayer 1850

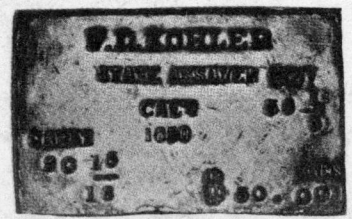

Ingots issued ranged from $36.55 to $150 .... RARE

PRIVATE GOLD

DUBOSQ & COMPANY

San Francisco 1850

1850 $5.00 .... $32,000
1850 $10.00 38,000

BALDWIN & COMPANY

San Francisco 1850

1850 $10.00 .... $10,000

1850 $5.00 .... $1,600
1851 $10.00 5,000
1851 $20.00 .... RARE

PRIVATE GOLD

SCHULTZ & COMPANY
San Francisco 1851

1851 $5.00 .... $9,000

DUNBAR & COMPANY
San Francisco 1851

1851 $5.00 .... RARE

WASS, MOLITOR & COMPANY
San Francisco 1852-1855

1852 $5.00	$1,750
1852 $10.00	1,000
1855 $10.00	3,000
1855 $20.00	3,750
1855 $50.00	8,500

PRIVATE GOLD

KELLOGG & COMPANY

San Francisco 1854-1855

1854 $20.00 .... $900.00
1855 $20.00 1,000

1855 $50.00 .... RARE

OREGON EXCHANGE COMPANY

Oregon City, 1849

1849 $5.00 .... $4,000
1849 $10.00 13,500

PRIVATE GOLD

MORMON GOLD PIECES
Salt Lake City, Utah 1849-1860

1849	$2.50	$1,200
1849	$5.00	1,000
1849	$10.00	40,000
1849	$20.00	13,500

1850 $5.00 .... $1,000

1860 $5.00 .... $3,000

COLORADO GOLD PIECES
Clark, Gruber & Co. — Denver 1860-1861

1860 $10.00 .... $1,400
1860 $20.00 10,000

PRIVATE GOLD

CLARK, GRUBER & COMPANY

1860	$2.50	$450.00
1861	$2.50	475.00
1860	$5.00	600.00
1861	$5.00	600.00
1861	$10.00	800.00
1861	$20.00	3,500

JOHN PARSONS & COMPANY
Tarryall Mines — Colorado 1861

1861	$2.50	RARE
1861	$5.00	RARE

J. J. CONWAY & COMPANY
Georgia Gulch, Colorado, 1861

1861	$2.50	$35,000
1861	$5.00	40,000
1861	$10.00	RARE

UNITED STATES PAPER MONEY

Large Size Notes: Some people today still remember the old, large size, "horse-blanket" currency in everyday use until 1929. By then paper money was taken for granted, but the public was very distrustful when the government introduced its own emissions in 1861 because of the Civil War. The value of such notes (called Greenbacks because of the backs printed in green) rose and fell with the tides of war. Stability came only after the war ended, and by the mid-1860's a variety of notes could be found in circulation.

Large size United States paper money consists of about 140 designs and many varieties. There are twelve major classes of notes. These vary according to the specific backing used for the issue, or other aspects of authorization. Examples: National Bank Notes, Legal Tender Notes, Treasury Notes, Refunding Certificates, Gold or Silver Certificates.

Modern Size Notes: These are the notes we use today. The change from the old, large size to our modern size came about not only because of the added convenience but also because it meant a great cost saving to the government. More notes could be printed at one time, and they were easier to work with and handle. On July 10, 1929, the first reduced size notes were placed into circulation.

Six different major types of modern size notes have been made: Legal Tender or United States Notes (red seal), Silver Certificates (blue seal), National Currency (brown seal), Federal Reserve Bank Notes (brown seal), Federal Reserve Notes (green seal), and Gold Certificates (gold seal). Today over 99% of our paper money consists of Federal Reserve Notes, but in past years all of the above types were in daily circulation. Through these notes one may see the changes wrought by the Great Depression, World War II (special printings and overprints), and newer printing techniques. Recent changes include the addition of the motto "In God We Trust" to all notes starting in 1957, and the $2 Bicentennial issue.

Collecting Modern Size Notes: It often comes as a surprise that there are many issues which command substantial premiums. Many factors are responsible for this: collectors were not abundant in the 1920's and 1930's, the Depression was on and not many notes were saved, and some issues were very small while others were recalled (Gold Certificates). Representatives of all six major types may be obtained easily.

UNITED STATES NOTES — Red Seal

United States Notes, also known as Legal Tender Notes or Greenbacks, were first authorized by the Act of Congress of February 25, 1862. Denominations for the large-size notes ranged from $1 to $10,000. Modern-size notes are presently being issued only in the $100 denomination, as delivery of $2 notes was terminated in July of 1965 and $5 in November of 1967. The $1 Series of 1928 was released mainly in Puerto Rico years after the notes were printed, but it is no longer in circulation.

When finished, United States Notes are delivered to a vault under custody of the Treasurer of the United States. As required by the Act of May 31, 1878, and the recently enacted Old Series Currency Adjustment Act, the amount outstanding is kept at $322,681,016. The seal and serial numbers are in red.

1 Dollar Note

Series	Signatures	Avg. Dealers Pay	Average Retail Prices VF	Unc.
1928	Woods-Woodin	$12.00	$20.00	$95.00

UNITED STATES NOTES — Red Seal

2 Dollar Notes

Series	Signatures	Avg. Dealers Pay	Average Retail Prices	
			VF	Unc.
1928	Tate-Mellon	$6.00	$10.00	$25.00
1928-A	Woods-Mellon	14.00	25.00	95.00
1928-B	Woods-Mills	65.00	100.00	300.00
1928-C	Julian-Morgenthau	5.00	7.00	20.00
1928-D	Julian-Morgenthau	3.00	5.00	15.00
1928-E	Julian-Vinson	4.50	10.00	30.00
1928-F	Julian-Snyder	4.00	5.00	15.00
1928-G	Clark-Snyder	2.00	3.00	10.00

2 Dollar Notes

Series	Signatures			
1953	Priest-Humphrey	...	...	4.50
1953-A	Priest-Anderson	...	...	4.00
1953-B	Smith-Dillon	...	...	4.00
1953-C	Granahan-Dillon	...	...	3.50
1963	Granahan-Dillon	...	...	3.00
1963-A	Granahan-Fowler	...	...	3.00

UNITED STATES NOTES — Red Seal

5 Dollar Notes

Series	Signatures	Avg. Dealers Pay	Average Retail Prices VF	Unc.
1928	Woods-Mellon	$6.00	$9.00	$23.00
1928-A	Woods-Mills	7.50	12.00	40.00
1928-B	Julian-Morgenthau	6.00	8.00	15.00
1928-C	Julian-Morgenthau	6.00	8.00	15.00
1928-D	Julian-Vinson	8.00	14.00	75.00
1928-E	Julian-Snyder	5.50	8.00	15.00
1928-F	Clark-Snyder	5.50	7.50	14.00
1953	Priest-Humphrey	5.50	7.00	10.00
1953-A	Priest-Anderson	...	...	7.50
1953-B	Smith-Dillon	...	...	7.50
1953-C	Granahan-Dillon	...	...	7.00
1963	Granahan-Dillon	...	...	6.00

100 Dollar Notes

Series	Signatures			
1966	Granahan-Fowler	...	...	140.00
1966-A	Elston-Kennedy	...	...	145.00

SILVER CERTIFICATES — Blue Seal

Certificates backed by silver dollars were first authorized by the Bland-Allison Act of February 28, 1878. Large-size notes were made in denominations from $1 to $1000.

Modern-size Silver Certificates were made only in the $1, $5 and $10 denominations. Upon completion they were delivered to a vault under the custody of the Treasurer of the United States. However, Silver Certificates are no longer being printed, as they were abolished by the Act of June 4, 1963 (at which time Federal Reserve $1 and $2 notes were authorized). The seal and series numbers are in blue.

1 Dollar Notes

Series	Signatures	Avg. Dealers Pay	Average Retail Prices VF	Unc.
1928	Tate-Mellon	$2.50	$4.00	$10.00
1928-A	Woods-Mellon	1.75	3.00	9.00
1928-B	Woods-Mills	1.75	3.00	9.00
1928-C	Woods-Woodin	50.00	100.00	275.00
1928-D	Julian-Woodin	45.00	75.00	200.00
1928-E	Julian-Morgenthau	150.00	275.00	625.00

| 1934 | Julian-Morgenthau | 1.50 | 3.50 | 9.50 |

SILVER CERTIFICATES — Blue Seal

Series	Signatures	Avg. Dealers Pay	Average Retail Prices	
			VF	Unc.
1935	Julian-Morgenthau	$1.50	$3.00	$11.00
1935-A	Julian-Morgenthau	...	...	4.50
1935-B	Julian-Vinson		3.00	11.00
1935-C	Julian-Snyder		2.00	5.50
1935-D	Clark-Snyder		...	5.00
1935-E	Priest-Humphrey		...	4.00
1935-F	Priest-Anderson		...	3.50
1935-G	Smith-Dillon		...	3.50

1935-G	Smith-Dillon (with motto)		...	5.00
1935-H	Granahan-Dillon		...	4.50
1957	Priest-Anderson		...	3.00
1957-A	Smith-Dillon		...	3.00
1957-B	Granahan-Dillon		...	3.00

SILVER CERTIFICATES — Blue Seal

5 Dollar Notes

Series	Signatures	Avg. Dealers Pay	Average Retail Prices	
			VF	Unc.
1934	Julian-Morgenthau	...	$7.00	$17.50
1934-A	Julian-Morgenthau	...	6.00	15.00
1934-B	Julian-Vinson	...	10.00	20.00
1934-C	Julian-Snyder	...	6.50	14.50
1934-D	Clark-Snyder	...	6.00	12.50
1953	Priest-Humphrey	...	...	14.00
1953-A	Priest-Anderson	...	...	10.00
1953-B	Smith-Dillon	...	...	10.00
1953-C	Granahan-Dillon	(not released)		

10 Dollar Notes

1933	Julian-Woodin	500.00	750.00	4,000
1933-A	Julian-Morgenthau	Unknown		
1934	Julian-Morgenthau	...	14.00	30.00
1934-A	Julian-Morgenthau	...	14.00	30.00
1934-B	Julian-Vinson	50.00	100.00	550.00
1934-C	Julian-Snyder	...	13.00	25.00
1934-D	Clark-Snyder	...	12.50	25.00
1953	Priest-Humphrey	...	12.50	30.00
1953-A	Priest-Anderson	...	12.50	25.00
1953-B	Smith-Dillon	...	12.50	30.00

NATIONAL CURRENCY — Brown Seal

Modern-size National Currency was first issued on July 15, 1929. Unusual features of this issue include the use of the Register-Treasurer signature combination (instead of Secretary-Treasurer as found on most other modern-size notes) and the series date which is 1929. The printing plates for the face side are also quite different from other modern-size types. The engraved borders are reduced in proportion and size to make room for the imprinting of bank names, locations, charter numbers and names of bank officials. The seal and serial numbers are in brown. The backs are uniform with other modern types. No star notes as such were made for the National Currency series.

There are two distinct types of modern-size National Currency. Type One, issued from July 1929 to May 1933, has the bank's charter number in two places, in black.

Type Two notes were issued from May 1933 to May 1935. These bore consecutive serial numbers, the suffix letters were dropped and the charter number of the bank was added twice more, in thinner brown numerals. Thus, the charter number appears four times on Type Two notes—twice in black logotype and twice in brown as described.

Type 1—Bank Number in Two Positions

Type 2—Bank Number in Four Positions

5 Dollar Notes

Series	Signatures	Avg. Dealers Pay	Average Retail Prices VF	Unc.
1929 Type 1	Jones-Woods	$12.50	$20.00	$45.00
1929 Type 2	Jones-Woods	15.00	23.00	55.00

NATIONAL CURRENCY — Brown Seal

Series	Signatures	Avg. Dealers Pay	Average Retail Prices VF	Unc.
10 Dollar Notes				
1929 Type 1	Jones-Woods	$12.50	$24.00	$50.00
1929 Type 2	Jones-Woods	14.00	25.00	55.00
20 Dollar Notes				
1929 Type 1	Jones-Woods	22.50	32.00	55.00
1929 Type 2	Jones-Woods	22.50	33.00	57.50
50 Dollar Notes				
1929 Type 1	Jones-Woods	55.00	75.00	150.00
1929 Type 2	Jones-Woods	57.50	80.00	160.00
100 Dollar Notes				
1929 Type 1	Jones-Woods	110.00	130.00	215.00
1929 Type 2	Jones-Woods	115.00	140.00	225.00

These valuations are for the most common varieties of each denomination and type. Scarcity varies greatly between banks and states of issue, and in each case the more difficult to acquire issues may be valued higher than the prices listed.

FEDERAL RESERVE BANK NOTES — Brown Seal

These notes very closely resembled the National Currency issues; alterations were made only in the overprint on the face side. The designated letter of each Federal Reserve Bank and District was placed on the notes in four places. The brown seal was slightly larger than that used on the National Bank notes, and words OR BY LIKE DEPOSIT OF OTHER SECURITIES were logotyped near the top. The series date remained 1929 and the engraved signatures of Jones and Woods (Register and Treasurer) were also retained.

Serial numbers for each Federal Reserve Bank started with 00000001A, preceded by a District letter A to L used as a prefix.

Federal Reserve Bank Notes denominations included $5, $10, $20, $50, and $100. Their issuance was discontinued in

FEDERAL RESERVE BANK NOTES — Brown Seal

July, 1935; however, during World War II (1942) and a temporary shortage of currency, additional supplies of these Bank Notes were released from storage and charged out as Federal Reserve Notes.

5 Dollar Notes

Series	District	Avg. Dealers Pay	Average Retail Prices VF	Unc.
1929	Boston	$6.50	$15.00	$45.00
1929	New York	6.00	12.00	40.00
1929	Philadelphia	6.50	15.00	45.00
1929	Cleveland	6.00	12.00	40.00
1929	Richmond		Not Issued	
1929	Atlanta	6.50	15.00	85.00
1929	Chicago	6.00	10.00	35.00
1929	St. Louis	50.00	100.00	500.00
1929	Minneapolis	7.00	20.00	100.00
1929	Kansas City	6.00	12.00	60.00
1929	Dallas	6.50	15.00	45.00
1929	San Francisco	375.00	500.00	RARE

10 Dollar Notes

Series	District			
1929	Boston	11.50	20.00	47.50
1929	New York	11.00	16.00	42.50
1929	Philadelphia	11.00	18.00	50.00
1929	Cleveland	11.00	18.00	45.00
1929	Richmond	11.50	22.00	55.00
1929	Atlanta	11.50	20.00	55.00
1929	Chicago	11.00	18.00	42.50
1929	St. Louis	11.00	18.00	55.00
1929	Minneapolis	12.00	30.00	85.00
1929	Kansas City	11.50	20.00	60.00
1929	Dallas	15.00	45.00	225.00
1929	San Francisco	12.50	40.00	100.00

FEDERAL RESERVE BANK NOTES — Brown Seal

Series	District	Avg. Dealers Pay	Average Retail Prices VF	Unc.
		20 Dollar Notes		
1929	Boston	...	...	$90.00
1929	New York	...	...	55.00
1929	Philadelphia	...	...	60.00
1929	Cleveland	...	...	60.00
1929	Richmond	...	...	62.50
1929	Atlanta	...	...	65.00
1929	Chicago	...	...	55.00
1929	St. Louis	...	$40.00	100.00
1929	Minneapolis	...	...	70.00
1929	Kansas City	...	...	80.00
1929	Dallas	25.00	60.00	175.00
1929	San Francisco	...	35.00	90.00

Series	District			
		50 Dollar Notes		
1929	Boston		Not Issued	
1929	New York	...	65.00	150.00
1929	Philadelphia		Not Issued	
1929	Cleveland	...	65.00	150.00
1929	Richmond		Not Issued	
1929	Atlanta		Not Issued	
1929	Chicago	...	70.00	150.00
1929	St. Louis		Not Issued	
1929	Minneapolis	...	90.00	200.00
1929	Kansas City	...	75.00	200.00
1929	Dallas	...	80.00	225.00
1929	San Francisco	...	70.00	200.00

Series	District			
		100 Dollar Notes		
1929	Boston		Not Issued	
1929	New York	...	...	200.00
1929	Philadelphia		Not Issued	
1929	Cleveland	...	...	210.00
1929	Richmond	...	...	250.00
1929	Atlanta		Not Issued	
1929	Chicago	...	...	200.00
1929	St. Louis		Not Issued	
1929	Minneapolis	...	...	245.00
1929	Kansas City	110.00	125.00	280.00
1929	Dallas	110.00	200.00	Scarce
1929	San Francisco		Not Issued	

FEDERAL RESERVE NOTES

Modern-size Federal Reserve Notes were first issued in 1929, series dated 1928. Denominations range from $1 to $10,000. Those of $500 and higher were discontinued by action of the Board of Governors of the Federal Reserve System on June 26, 1946; on July 14, 1969, they were retired from circulation, but a few are still held in banks.

The twelve Federal Reserve Banks are organized and operate for public service as authorized by Congress. They are under supervision of the Board of Governors of the Federal Reserve System, an agency of the Federal Government.

Federal Reserve Banks release these notes according to the needs of their regions. One can easily tell which Bank issued a particular note by examining its face side. A number and corresponding letter were assigned to each of the Federal Reserve Districts, and both have been used on the notes in various combinations. At present a Bank seal to the left of the portrait carries the letter (and the name of the Bank); this same letter serves as the prefix letter for every serial number on all notes issued by the respective Bank. The District number is imprinted in four places, also on the face of the note. The Treasury seal and serial numbers are in green.

1 Dollar Notes

Series	Signatures	Average Retail Prices Unc.
1963	Granahan-Dillon	$3.00
1963A	Granahan-Fowler	2.75
1963B	Granahan-Barr	3.00
1969	Elston-Kennedy	2.50
1969A	Kabis-Kennedy	2.50
1969B	Kabis-Connally	2.00
1969C	Bañuelos-Connally	2.00
1969D	Bañuelos-Shultz	1.75
1974	Neff-Simon	1.25
1977	Morton-Blumenthal	(current)
1977A	Morton-Miller	(current)

FEDERAL RESERVE NOTES

2 Dollar Notes

Series	Signatures	Average Retail Prices Unc.
1976	Neff-Simon	(Current)

5 Dollar Notes

1928	Tate-Mellon	$35.00
1928A	Woods-Mellon	32.50
1928B	Woods-Mellon	30.00
1928C	Woods-Mills	400.00
1928D	Woods-Woodin	Scarce
1934	Julian-Morgenthau	20.00
1934A	Julian-Morgenthau	20.00
1934B	Julian-Vinson	20.00
1934C	Julian-Snyder	17.50
1934D	Clark-Snyder	15.00
1950	Clark-Snyder	13.00
1950A	Priest-Humphrey	12.50
1950B	Priest-Anderson	12.00
1950C	Smith-Dillon	11.50
1950D	Granahan-Dillon	10.00
1950E	Granahan-Fowler	11.50
1963	Granahan-Dillon	10.00
1963A	Granahan-Fowler	8.00
1969	Elston-Kennedy	7.00
1969A	Kabis-Connally	6.00
1969B	Bañuelos-Connally	6.00
1969C	Bañuelos-Shultz	6.00
1974	Neff-Simon	(current)
1977	Morton-Blumenthal	(current)
1977A	Morton-Miller	(current)

FEDERAL RESERVE NOTES

10 Dollar Notes

Series	Signatures	Average Retail Prices Unc.
1928	Tate-Mellon	$30.00
1928A	Woods-Mellon	27.50
1928B	Woods-Mellon	25.00
1928C	Woods-Mills	35.00
1934	Julian-Morgenthau	20.00
1934A	Julian-Morgenthau	20.00
1934B	Julian-Vinson	20.00
1934C	Julian-Snyder	20.00
1934D	Clark-Snyder	20.00
1950	Clark-Snyder	18.00
1950A	Priest-Humphrey	17.50
1950B	Priest-Anderson	15.00
1950C	Smith-Dillon	15.00
1950D	Granahan-Dillon	13.50
1950E	Granahan-Fowler	14.00
1963	Granahan-Dillon	12.50
1963A	Granahan-Fowler	12.00
1969	Elston-Kennedy	11.00
1969A	Kabis-Connally	11.00
1969B	Bañuelos-Connally	11.00
1969C	Bañuelos-Shultz	11.00
1974	Neff-Simon	(current)
1977	Morton-Blumenthal	(current)
1977A	Morton-Miller	(current)

FEDERAL RESERVE NOTES

20 Dollar Notes

Series	Signatures	Average Retail Prices Unc.
1928	Tate-Mellon	$40.00
1928A	Woods-Mellon	40.00
1928B	Woods-Mellon	35.00
1928C	Woods-Mills	150.00
1934	Julian-Morgenthau	35.00
1934	Julian-Morgenthau	35.00
1934A	Julian-Morgenthau	35.00
1934B	Julian-Vinson	35.00
1934C	Julian-Snyder	35.00
1934D	Clark-Snyder	35.00
1950	Clark-Snyder	30.00
1950A	Priest-Humphrey	27.50
1950B	Priest-Anderson	27.50
1950C	Smith-Dillon	27.50
1950D	Granahan-Dillon	25.00
1950E	Granahan-Fowler	26.00
1963	Granahan-Dillon	24.00
1963A	Granahan-Fowler	23.00
1969	Elston-Kennedy	21.00
1969A	Kabis-Connally	21.00
1969B	Bañuelos-Connally	21.00
1969C	Bañuelos-Shultz	21.00
1974	Neff-Simon	(current)
1977	Morton-Blumenthal	(current)

50 Dollar Notes

Series	Signatures	
1928	Woods-Mellon	100.00
1928A	Woods-Mellon	90.00
1934	Julian-Morgenthau	60.00
1934A	Julian-Morgenthau	60.00
1934B	Julian-Vinson	60.00

FEDERAL RESERVE NOTES

		Average Retail Prices Unc.
1934C	Julian-Snyder	$60.00
1934D	Clark-Snyder	60.00
1950	Clark-Snyder	58.00
1950A	Priest-Humphrey	58.00
1950B	Priest-Anderson	58.00
1950C	Smith-Dillon	58.00
1950D	Granahan-Dillon	58.00
1950E	Granahan-Fowler	60.00
1963A	Granahan-Fowler	52.50
1969	Elston-Kennedy	52.50
1969A	Kabis-Connally	52.50
1969B	Bañuelos-Connally	52.50
1969C	Bañuelos-Shultz	52.50
1974	Neff-Simon	(current)
1977	Morton-Blumenthal	(current)

100 Dollar Notes

Series	Signatures	
1928	Woods-Mellon	185.00
1928A	Woods-Mellon	185.00
1934	Julian-Morgenthau	125.00
1934A	Julian-Morgenthau	125.00
1934B	Julian-Vinson	125.00
1934C	Julian-Snyder	125.00
1934D	Clark-Snyder	125.00
1950	Clark-Snyder	110.00
1950A	Priest-Humphrey	110.00
1950B	Priest-Anderson	110.00
1950C	Smith-Dillon	110.00
1950D	Granahan-Dillon	110.00
1950E	Granahan-Fowler	110.00
1963A	Granahan-Fowler	105.00
1969	Elston-Kennedy	105.00
1969A	Kabis-Connally	105.00
1969C	Bañuelos-Shultz	105.00
1974	Neff-Simon	(current)
1977	Morton-Blumenthal	(current)

GOLD CERTIFICATES — Gold Seal

The Gold Certificates Series of 1928 are "Gold Coin" notes, so stated on the face. No heading is found in the usual place at the top; instead, it is to the left of the portrait near the Treasury seal. The color of the seal and serial numbers is gold.

Series	Signatures	Avg. Dealers Pay	Average Retail Prices VF	Unc.
		10 Dollar Notes		
1928	Woods-Mellon	$13.50	$25.00	$130.00
		20 Dollar Notes		
1928	Woods-Mellon	25.00	32.50	185.00
		50 Dollar Notes		
1928	Woods-Mellon	55.00	90.00	300.00
		100 Dollar Notes		
1928	Woods-Mellon	110.00	140.00	400.00

Higher denominations are extremely rare.

WORLD WAR II ISSUES
The Yellow Seal Silver Certificates

These were issued in North Africa during operations there in 1942. Later they were issued briefly at the beginning of the Sicilian campaign.

All bear the Julian-Morgenthau signature combination. Though the Treasury seals were printed in yellow, the serial numbers retained their usual blue color.

		1 Dollar Notes		
1935A	Julian-Morgenthau	4.00	7.50	50.00
		5 Dollar Notes		
1934A	Julian-Morgenthau	7.00	12.50	75.00
		10 Dollar Notes		
1934	Julian-Morgenthau	450.00	650.00	RARE
1934A	Julian-Morgenthau	12.00	16.50	85.00

THE HAWAII OVERPRINTS — Brown Seal

In July of 1942, specially marked U.S. currency was introduced in Hawaii as an economic defense measure against a possible Japanese invasion. If these notes had fallen into enemy hands, they could have been isolated easily and declared valueless. The notes are overprinted HAWAII face and back as illustrated. They also contain brown seals and serial numbers. All bear the Julian-Morgenthau signature combination. $1 notes are Silver Certificates; all the rest are San Francisco Federal Reserve Notes.

Series	Signatures	Avg. Dealers Pay	Average Retail Prices VF	Unc.
		1 Dollar Notes		
1935A	Julian-Morgenthau	$3.00	$6.50	$50.00
		5 Dollar Notes		
1934	Julian-Morgenthau	12.50	20.00	160.00
1934A	Julian-Morgenthau	7.50	14.00	120.00
		10 Dollar Notes		
1934A	Julian-Morgenthau	12.00	20.00	140.00
		20 Dollar Notes		
1934	Julian-Morgenthau	50.00	110.00	550.00
1934A	Julian-Morgenthau	22.50	35.00	275.00

WORLD WAR II ISSUES

Experimental "R" and "S" $1.00 Silver Certificates

These notes were made during World War II to test the wearing qualities of regular and special paper. Equal quantities were overprinted on the face with a red R or S, in the position shown. All bear signatures of Julian-Morgenthau and are dated Series 1935 A.

The R and S overprints were made to determine whether a special kind of paper might wear better in circulation than the regular paper normally used. The "R" represented those notes made of regular paper and the "S" was for those notes made of the special paper. Results of the experiment were inconclusive and no change was made in the kind of paper used for U. S. currency.

Series	Signatures		Avg. Dealers Pay	Average Retail Prices	
				VF	Unc.
1 Dollar Notes		With Red R			
1935A	Julian-Morgenthau		$15.00	$30.00	$190.00
		With Red S			
1935A	Julian-Morgenthau		10.00	20.00	120.00

INDEX

Bicentennial Coinage	84, 97, 107
Books and Periodicals	6
Buying and Selling	7, 11
Civil War Tokens	11
Clad Coins	5
Classifying Coins — Condition	8, 16
Cleaning Coins	7
Collecting — How to Start	5
Colonial Coinage	19
Commemoratives — Gold	160
Commemoratives — Silver	141
Condition of Coins	7, 16
Dealers — How to Locate	3, 6
Dimes	58
Distinguishing Marks	9
Dollars — Gold	109
Dollars — Silver	98
Double Eagles ($20 Gold Pieces)	135
Eagles ($10 Gold Pieces)	128
Five Cent Nickels	44
Flying Eagle Cents	31
Foreign Coins	10
Gold	109
Grading of Condition	16
Half Cents	24
Half Dimes	54
Half Dollars	85
Half Eagles ($5 Gold Pieces)	120
Indian Head Cents	31
Introduction	3
Large Cents	27
Lettered Edge	27, 85, 98
Lincoln Cents	34

[191]

INDEX

Medals	10
Mint Marks — How to Locate	9
Mints	12
Numismatic Publications	6
One Dollar — Gold	109
Overdates	10
Paper Money	172
Preserving Coins	7
Private Gold Coins	162
Production of Coins	9
Proof Coins — How Made	13
Proof Coin Sets	14
Quarter Dollars	70
Quarter Eagles ($2.50 Gold Pieces)	112
Selling Coins	3, 7, 11
Special Mint Sets	15
Terms Used to Describe Coins	11
Three Cent Nickel	42
Three Cent Silver	43
Three Dollars — Gold	118
Tokens	10
Trade Dollars	102
Twenty Cent Pieces	70
Two Cent Pieces	41
Uncirculated Coins	8, 16
Unusual Coins	10
Valuation of Coins	3, 4, 5, 11
VDB — 1909 Cent Explanation	34